Teacher Appraisal
A Practical Guide

Professor E.C. Wragg
Director
School of Education
Exeter University

MACMILLAN EDUCATION

Related titles from Macmillan Education

Assessment: From Principles to Action
Robin-Lloyd Jones and Elizabeth Bray

Managing for Learning
John Buckley and David Styan

Preventive Approaches to Disruption
Barry Chisholm, David Kearney, Grenville Knight, Howard Little, Susan Morris and David Tweddle

Class Management and Control
E.C. Wragg

Handling Classroom Groups
Trevor Kerry and M.K. Sands

© E.C. Wragg 1987

All rights reserved. No reproduction, copy or transmission of this publication may be made without written permission.

No paragraph of this publication may be reproduced, copied or transmitted save with written permission or in accordance with the provisions of the Copyright Act 1956 (as amended), or under the terms of any licence permitting limited copying issued by the Copyright Licensing Agency, 33–4 Alfred Place, London WC1E 7DP.

Any person who does any unauthorised act in relation to this publication may be liable to criminal prosecution and civil claims for damages.

First published 1987
Reprinted 1988

Published by
MACMILLAN EDUCATION LTD
Houndmills, Basingstoke, Hampshire RG21 2XS
and London
Companies and representatives
throughout the world

Printed in Hong Kong

British Library Cataloguing in Publication Data
Wragg, E.C.
Teacher appraisal : a practical guide.
1. Teachers—Great Britain—Rating
of
I. Title
371.1′44′0941   LB2838
ISBN 0-333-45707-2

Contents **Introduction** v
Acknowledgements viii

Part 1   Issues in teacher appraisal 1

Defining the nature and purpose of appraisal 2
What is effective teaching? 4
Criteria for judging teachers 8
Appraisal within the context of school organisation 13
Closed or open appraisal? 20

Part 2   Methods of appraisal 22

Classroom observation 23
The role and effect of the observer 23
What to focus on in the classroom observation 25
Rating schedules and checklists 44
Peer appraisal and self-appraisal 50
Interviews 55
Using educational technology 58

Part 3   The implementation of teacher appraisal 60

The increasing scope of teachers' skills 60
Appraising senior staff 61
Differences between primary and secondary schools 64
Aftercare: in-service and professional development 66
Cost implications: time and money 68
Competent and incompetent teachers 70

Conclusion 76
Appendices 77
Bibliography 87

Activities	Activity 1	The purposes of appraisal	4
	Activity 2	What is good teaching?	11
	Activity 3	Classroom observation – what do we look for?	27
	Activity 4	Analysing and discussing a lesson	43
	Activity 5	Other perspectives, feedback from non-professionals	55
	Activity 6	A structure for appraisal	72

Introduction

The requirement in the 1986 Education Act that the performance of teachers should be regularly appraised provoked a mixed reaction. Some argued that appraisal already took place in that senior people in schools counsel their junior colleagues, write evaluative references about their teaching when they apply for posts elsewhere, or make judgements about whose work is of sufficient quality to justify internal promotion. Sir Keith Joseph, then Secretary of State for Education, acknowledged as much in a Radio 4 interview I did with him in January 1985, when he said:

> Appraisal is going on the whole while now. What I'm asking is that the appraisal should be more formalised.

For some teachers the proposals brought back unhappy memories of being shredded by a tutor during student teacher days, or, perhaps, of a visit from one of those more old-fashioned HMI, known as 'Black Ravens', who sat at the back of the class writing a great deal, communicating little, but creating a distinct feeling of impending doom.

The fear of a possible humiliation ritual is one that bedevils the act of appraisal wherever it takes place. For most professionals the job they do and the competence they believe they have are central pillars in their daily lives. Without these much of the purpose of their existence as well as their self-confidence would evaporate. The act of appraisal can force people to confront themselves in a way they would normally wish to avoid. Indeed many teachers have developed well-oiled defences for protecting themselves from the inevitable bruising which occurs when we discover we are not as nifty professionally as we would like to believe, or as we once were.

Equally, there are numerous teachers and Heads who set themselves such high standards that they cannot possibly meet them. Psychiatrists and clinical psychologists who have dealt with teachers suffering from severe stress, or even breakdown, frequently have to help them establish fresh goals that are more realistic and have a chance of being achieved. Those responsible for appraisal must recognise that it is not always, therefore, a case of pushing expectations ever higher.

Down in the saloon bar of the 'Dog and Partridge', however, no such complexities exist. In the minds of many members of the public, legitimately concerned about the quality of schooling their children receive, teacher appraisal is unproblematic. Surely, it is argued, everyone knows who the good and bad teachers are. Therefore, some senior person in the school, presumably the Head, should simply give a pat on the head and a bonus to those who are especially competent, and kick, fire, or slip something into the cocoa of those who are not.

Somewhere in between the understandable, if oversimplified, quest for quality amongst lay people and the sometimes excessive angst generated by professionals, there must lie numerous sensible and sensitive ways of counselling teachers about their work and helping them improve their professional skills and the quality of their pupils' learning. That is why in this guide I shall not be concocting a single omni-purpose British Standard Appraisal Kit, but rather describing and analysing some of the many issues and approaches which may be considered by those involved in appraisal, whether as perpetrators or recipients.

There are background factors to be considered, such as what constitutes effective teaching, the implications of appraisal for relationships within organisations such as schools, and how other professions evaluate and nurture competence. I shall also try to analyse the specific techniques frequently applied: the use and misuse of rating schedules, behavioural checklists and some of the numerous approaches to classroom observation. There is also the question of the personalities involved: who should appraise whom; should it be insiders only, or is an external vantage point necessary; is it inescapably a superior–subordinate activity, or can people of equal status work collaboratively?

Another important issue is the matter of aftercare, vital but costly if teachers are to be given proper in-service support following an appraisal, rather than merely a grade or a brief comment. Then there is the thorny question of incompetent teachers, those found to be incapable of doing their job properly, an embarrassment to their colleagues but well protected by Unfair Dismissals legislation.

It is unlikely that I shall address all these issues in such a short guide to the satisfaction of every reader, but there are suggestions for further reading on page 87. There are also several activities such as may be useful for in-service courses or staff or governors' discussions. Since readers may include lay people such as governors, parents, politicians or others interested in appraisal, as well as teachers, heads, advisers, teacher trainers and administrators who work professionally in education, I have kept specialist terminology and footnotes to the minimum. I have also tried to follow non-sexist guidelines by using 'teachers' in the plural wherever possible and mixing 'he' and 'she' when not.

For those who are curious, my qualifications for writing this guide are first of all that I have been involved in the training of novice and experienced teachers for 21 years, second that I have three children in education, so like other parents I am concerned that they and their fellows enjoy the best teaching we can provide, third that my major research interest is classroom interaction, so I have watched and evaluated hundreds of lessons as part of research projects or teacher training programmes, and fourth that, like most others, I too bleed when I am appraised.

I once read through 180 written appraisals of courses I had taught to pupils aged 15 to 18. Something like 179 of these ranged from 'above average' to 'very good'. The 180th began, 'The trouble with you is that you think you are God's gift to teaching, and what makes you think your jokes are actually funny?' The temptation to crawl away into a quiet corner and plan a dignified suicide was overwhelming.

I hope I can make a contribution to appraisal being done well rather than in a ham-fisted way. If badly conceived and executed it will have a negative effect on teachers' morale and competence. It will require immense interpersonal skill from those involved in it, in whatever role, if it is to lead to the real improvements that will benefit pupils, parents and practitioners themselves.

Finally a note about terminology. In the pamphlet *Quality in Schools: Evaluation and Appraisal*, published by the Department of Education and Science in 1985, there is a proposal that terms should be used as follows:

(i)   *evaluation* – a general term used to describe any activity by the institution or the LEA where the quality of provision is the subject of systematic study;
(ii) *review* – a retrospective activity implying the collection and examination of evidence and information;
(iii) *appraisal* – emphasising the forming of qualitative judgements about an activity, a person or an organisation;
(iv) *assessment* – implying the use of measurement and/or grading based on known criteria.

A further comment was made about the use of the term *staff appraisal* including 'qualitative judgements about performance' and *staff development* being concerned with 'general matters of in-service training needs and career development' which may, of course, be based on staff appraisal.

In this guide I have used the terms in a similar way, but I have not made the qualitative/quantitative distinction between 'appraisal' and 'assessment' suggested above.

Ted Wragg
September 1987

Acknowledgements

The author and publishers wish to thank the following who have kindly given permission for the use of copyright material.

American Psychological Association for adapted material from 'The Development and evaluation of behaviourally based rating scales' by J. P. Campbell, M. D. Dunette, R. D. Arvey and L. V. Hellervik, *Journal of Applied Psychology*, 57.
Edward Arnold (Publishers) Ltd for material from *Managing Human Resources* by A. G. Cowling and C. J. B. Mailer, 1981.
Croom Helm Ltd for material from *Classroom Teaching Skills* by E. C. Wragg, 1984.
The Controller of Her Majesty's Stationery Office for Crown copyright material.

Every effort has been made to trace all the copyright holders but if any have been inadvertently overlooked the publishers will be pleased to make the necessary arrangement at the first opportunity.

The cartoons on pages 17, 25, 39 and 72 were drawn by Jonathan Hall.

Part 1 Issues in teacher appraisal

The demand for a formal system of teacher appraisal must be seen as part of a general push for accountability. In any activity involving the expenditure of large sums of private or public money, the sponsors are likely to ask for an account to be rendered, especially if financial resources are tight. Education costs billions of pounds, and even though teachers may not always be as well paid as they deserve, salaries do constitute a significant proportion of that expenditure.

Furthermore, at a time when millions of jobs have disappeared, in most cases never to return in their previous form, parents recognise that the more highly educated in society have a better chance of obtaining employment than those who leave school with few or no formal qualifications. Hence the increasing pressure on schools during the 1970s, and especially during the 1980s, to achieve as much as possible during the compulsory years of education.

With the political emphasis very much on financial aspects of education it is not surprising that the language of accountancy is not far from discussions about effectiveness. Thus terms like 'cost effective' or 'performance indicators', which sometimes do not fit well with the traditionally held view of teaching as an art surrounded by a certain amount of mystique, are increasingly heard during discussions about education. With millions of pupils and hundreds of thousands of teachers it is tempting to think entirely in terms of *quantities*: whether the teacher is in the top 10 per cent, obtains high marks from raters, or achieves large numbers of exam successes from pupils. Quantitative aspects do have a part to play, but there is a very strong qualitative dimension to be considered.

In addition to the difficulties caused by unemployment and parental pressure, teachers are now compared, unfairly, with the finest communicators in the world. A lesson in a primary school on insects may be judged in the eyes of the pupils alongside a television programme such as *Life on Earth* presented by David Attenborough. Not only is he an outstanding teacher, but he also has access to the most brilliantly and expensively filmed vignettes of insect life from a galaxy of photographers and naturalists all over the globe. The jobbing teacher with a few worksheets, wallcharts, filmstrips and dehydrated butterflies can easily look pedestrian in comparison with the glossy images of the high-budget television series. The final version of a recorded television programme may be Take 36 for all the viewer knows, but live teaching is always Take 1.

Defining the nature and purpose of appraisal

How people define and apply appraisal will depend on their own attitudes and values. Those who believe teaching to be a refuge for life's incompetents will see it as a way of smoking out the indolent and incapable. Many who actually work in education will regard it as part of a continuous process for the improvement and extension of professional skills. Such a view sees any individual act of appraisal as an interim measure, both retrospective and prospective, looking back at what has or has not been achieved, taking stock of the present, and then planning some pathway that will help the teacher develop further in the future. Thus the notion of appraisal, on the surface a neutral concept, can acquire overtones of retribution or support, depending on the individual's vantage point.

Another person with a strong financial perspective would see it as a value-for-money exercise, addressing the question, 'Is whatever teacher X does a better investment of money than, say, buying micro-computers, books, ancillary helpers, films, videocassettes, and all the other things a teacher's salary might purchase?' This view would also encompass a comparative dimension and seek to compare teachers with each other to discover which appear to give a greater return on their salary. It is a perspective which may be accorded a higher profile by Heads given more autonomy over all the resources, human and material, in their school.

In industry the term commonly used is 'performance appraisal'. The word 'performance' carries with it both industrial associations of products and profits, as well as theatrical notions of someone centre stage enacting a scene before an audience. There is some reluctance amongst teachers to being perceived either as an intermediary in a simple input-output industrial model, or as someone obliged to dominate the classroom when under observation because of pressure to 'perform'. A few years ago there was considerable embarrassment in initial teacher training when heavy-weight external examiners with a secondary school background, mistakenly turned loose to watch primary student teachers, subsequently announced that they were unable to judge what they had seen because the teacher had not 'performed'.

Despite these difficulties over terminology there is some value in looking at the purposes of appraisal in industry and commerce, and Judith Whyte (1986) has written a full review of assessment objectives and procedures in these fields. One principal purpose commonly reported is the linking of monetary rewards and job performance, a controversial issue in teaching but one which is likely to be built increasingly into salary settlements. Others frequently mentioned include facilitating the more effective use of human and material resources, identifying candidates for promotion to higher responsibility, improving individuals' motivation, dismissing or demoting the incompetent, rationalising and redeploying employees, and, though this is rarely stated in explicit form, exercising control over staff. Sir David Hancock, Permanent Secretary at the Department of Education and Science, echoed some of these sentiments when he said the DES wished to 'apply to the teaching force standards of management which have become common elsewhere'. He wanted soundly based decisions on such matters as staff deployment, in-service training, promotion and career development.

One way of confronting the question about objectives in appraisal is to think of each of the various individuals and interest groups. For many people the principal purpose will be to improve the quality of pupil learning, and in this respect the interests of children can coincide closely with the professional development needs of teachers. This view will put a premium on classroom observation and the analysis of classroom processes. One can then focus on teachers and the wider demands made of them: for example, the need to keep up to date in their own specialist field or, in the case of those, especially in primary schools, who require good general knowledge, several subject areas; their involvement in extra-curricular activities; liaison with parents, governors and the local community; the need to understand any difficulties which might be faced by children from different social and ethnic groups, those with special educational needs. If another principal purpose then is to help teachers improve their understanding of and competence in these wider aspects of their job, they might need to study further, undertake a piece of systematic enquiry, visit and talk to community leaders, go to other schools, interview parents, or take an in-service course.

One important way of ensuring that appraisal is not rejected out of hand is for teachers to feel involved in the processes and decision making. I shall be describing at various points in this guide some activities which are set out clearly in box form on the relevant page, and which might be undertaken by teachers within their own school or during in-service courses, or by governors and others who are involved with schools. Most of these activities are simple to organise and require nothing more than a small group of people and 30 to 90 minutes of time.

The first of these is about the purposes of appraisal. It is simply an agenda for discussion, and someone should chair the group through the sub-headings. Where several small groups are meeting, a plenary session to compare the views of each group would be useful. The exercise can help a school begin to plan its appraisal policy and code of practice. It is possible, of course, that some teachers may fold their arms and say 'The only reason for appraisal is that we have to do it by law'. Though it will be tempting for the group chairman to say that such members must not pass Go and will not collect their £200, it is worth urging them to participate in the discussion because they will be able to express their reservations under 1(b), 2 and 4 of Activity 1.

Activity 1   **The purposes of appraisal**

1. (a) What good purposes of appraisal can the group devise?
   (b) What bad purposes or misuse would the group wish to avoid?
2. What does the group think of the following commonly cited purposes:
   (a) To identify teachers who might one day be promoted;
   (b) To improve teachers' classroom skills;
   (c) To determine what further professional training teachers need;
   (d) To decide who should be given greater salary rewards;
   (e) To deal more effectively with incompetent teachers;
   (f) To help (i) deploy teachers most sensibly according to the school's needs and their talents,
   (ii) redeploy teachers sensitively should the need arise;
   (g) To determine whether the school's policies are being implemented.
3. Decide whether there are any goals about which the group has some degree of consensus, and then discuss what sort of appraisal procedures would best suit these aims.
4. Decide whether there are any anxieties about appraisal within the group and discuss how, and indeed if, these should be assuaged.

What is effective teaching?   One assumption built into the notion of appraisal is that we know what effective teaching is and can recognise it when we see it, or obversely that we can identify ineffective teaching and take steps to make it more effective. At an individual level this is probably true in that we all have our personal views about teaching and can defend them quite persuasively.

Unfortunately, the consensus which was thought to obtain in the nineteenth century, when training institutions were called 'Normal Schools' on the grounds that there was some commonly agreed 'norm' of good teaching, no longer exists. One only has to think of the quarrels about so-called traditional and progressive teaching styles, the argument over teaching sign language to deaf children, the many methods of teaching reading, each with its adherents and critics, the debate about the systematic teaching of grammar in English lessons, the use of a predominantly oral approach in foreign language teaching, or the pros and cons of playing the role of neutral chairman during discussion of contentious issues, to realise that, in a pluralist and argumentative society like our own, no single stereotype is supreme.

There is also the pressing question about what exactly is meant by 'effective'. For some it is strictly about what children learn, and the more they absorb the more effective the teacher. Others would argue that incremental gains in pupils' learning are only one part of the story, and that the real test is approval by those competent to judge: pupils, heads, experienced observers, fellow teachers.

There is no guaranteed agreement here either. Teachers may judge their fellows by their acceptability or otherwise as a staffroom colleague, and in many cases have never actually witnessed them teaching, whereas pupils see them every day in the classroom, but rarely in a social context. Heads are often dependent on indirect evidence such as plaudits or complaints from parents, the sound or absence of noise from their classroom, and more visible features such as punctuality, dress, behaviour at staff meetings, report writing, or contribution to out-of-school activities. There are also significant differences between primary and secondary schools. In open-plan primary schools, or where the Head makes a practice of teaching alongside other teachers, professional competence or lack of it will be much more public than in a secondary school where most teachers operate fairly privately inside their own box classroom.

There are numerous significant differences between teaching and industrial processes. In teaching there is no *single* agreed outcome. In professional football the major objectives are to score goals and avoid conceding them; in many businesses the principal intention is to sell as many products as possible with maximum profits for shareholders and the minimum of complaints about poor quality from purchasers; doctors try to cure as many patients as they can, and dentists seek to reduce tooth decay and avoid the unnecessary loss of teeth in their patients. Teachers on the other hand are often given numerous responsibilities, some specific and tangible like teaching basic skills in a range of fields in the primary phase, or specialist subjects like mathematics, science and foreign languages at the secondary stage, others vague like 'developing responsible adults for the world of the twenty-first century', 'realising the full potential of every child', or fostering something as important but elusive as 'happiness'. Since children are influenced by their families, their friends, other adults and the mass media it is not easy, either, to assign credit or blame should these more vague hopes materialise or fail to come about.

Judging achievement in many fields of endeavour is much easier. The football team which wins consistently, unless it resorts to underhand methods, has clearly been more successful than the one which loses regularly; sales figures, profits, number of products rejected during quality control, complaints from customers, volume of repairs needed under guarantee, are all valuable indicators of 'effectiveness' in the commercial world. Furthermore many professional skills can be produced to order. Ask a professional musician to play the violin, time an international sprinter over 100 metres, or watch a glassblower for a few seconds and the skills are immediately obvious and demonstrable. Teaching skill on the other hand is rarely so explosive. Much of it may be painstaking, for stayers rather than sprinters. The show-off who can produce a one-off flashy lesson when observed may be less valuable and effective with a class of children over a whole year than the quieter, less extrovert teacher who is deeply interested in individuals, marks their work meticulously and sustains the effort over several months.

During the 1950s there was a considerable amount of energy devoted to seeking the ideal teacher stereotype. Teachers were rated by observers, tests were given, pupils were polled, Heads were quizzed. An American writer, Barr (1961), summarised a massive amount of this work by concluding:

> Some teachers were preferred by administrators, some were liked by pupils, and some taught in classes where there were substantial pupil gains, and generally speaking these were not the same teachers.
> There is plenty of evidence to indicate that different practitioners observing the same teacher teach, or studying data about her, may arrive at very different evaluations of her; this observation is equally true of the evaluation experts; starting with different approaches, and using different data-gathering devices, they, too, arrive at very different evaluations.

More recent classroom research, especially in the United States, has begun to claim a degree of consistency. Nate Gage (1978) in his book *The Scientific Basis of the Art of Teaching* argues that the majority of systematic studies of children in the early years of schooling now show that, so far as the development of basic skills in such fields as reading and arithmetic is concerned, teachers who teach in what many would call a 'formal' style, that is with more teacher direction, less pupil movement permitted, more testing of achievement, appear to obtain better test scores than those who adopt a 'progressive' approach with greater informality and more pupil decision making.

This sounds, on the surface, as if the quest for models of effectiveness is over. Urge everyone to teach this way, it could be argued, and reading and arithmetic competence will soar. Yet if one looks at many of the studies which try to relate what teachers do in the classroom to what pupils actually learn the problem becomes clear immediately. Most research is based on tests of short-term memory, whereas many teachers have longer-term objectives. Thus the music teacher, hoping her pupils will enjoy and practise music throughout their lives, may well find herself formally assessed in terms of whether or not they know what a minim is or can beat 4/4 time, which may or may not be related to life-long interest.

An American study by Guetzkow (1954) showed how easily inferences can be made about the effectiveness of teaching on short-term, easily measured criteria alone. A first-year group of students studying psychology as part of a general course at the University of Michigan was divided into three groups. The first group was given a lecture course and regular tests, the other two groups were in tutorial and discussion groups. At the end of the course the students in the lecture/testing group obtained superior scores to the other groups of students in the final examination, chalking up what looks to be a victory for didactic teaching. However, when the investigators decided to follow up the cohort of students three years later, what they found was especially interesting. Not one student from the lecture course had chosen to major in psychology, but 14 members of the discussion/tutorial groups had done so. On short-term criteria (test scores) the lecture approach was most 'effective', but on longer-term criteria (interest, motivation, the desire to study to a higher level) it was the tutorial and discussion approach which had more impact.

The messages seem to be clear enough when one is considering the question of effective teaching:

- There is no single way of teaching well. Many different styles find favour according to circumstances.
- There will be differences of opinion even amongst those highly experienced in the profession.

- Effectiveness as a teacher extends beyond the boundaries of the classroom and preparation and planning, pastoral care, relationships with others such as fellow teachers and parents must be taken into account.
- Systematic studies of teachers often use short-term scores based on what can be readily measured. A longer-term perspective must also be considered.

Criteria for judging teachers

The lack of hard empirical evidence about effective teaching means that there is no easy solution to be discovered in the research literature, though certain findings and many of the procedures used by researchers will be of interest to those involved in teacher appraisal. There will, therefore, be a strong subjective element when judgements and decisions are made. In some cases it will be power and status or intuition and whim that determine what these should be, rather than research evidence or the rights and wrongs of any particular case.

In the United States during the 1970s and 1980s there has been a great deal of interest and activity in developing prescriptive training courses for teachers. In one of these developed by a specialist teacher education research and development institute one of the 'undesirable' pieces of behaviour by teachers was thought to be repeating a pupil's answer. Whole new training packages were devised to ensure that teachers spent less time repeating what pupils had just said. Unfortunately, however, another similar research and development institute in another part of the United States decided that repeating a pupil's answer was a good thing, and so it developed rival packages to achieve the opposite effect.

It is important that the views and perceptions of the people centrally involved in appraisal should be taken into account when any systematic approach is devised. In one school a checklist was devised with the item 'Teacher sticks to lesson plan' as a positive hurrah criterion of effectiveness. It was the view of the Head that it was desirable to keep to one's initial plan. I have seen enough disastrous lessons over the years because teachers insisted on adhering to their plan, even when the fidgeting, restlessness and misbehaviour of the class shrieked for a change of activity, to know that inflexibility can also have a negative effect. Keeping to or altering one's lesson plan is a perfectly legitimate topic for discussion after a teacher has been observed, but not solely in terms of it being exclusively desirable or undesirable, irrespective of circumstances, and simply because someone in authority has rigid views on the matter.

The question of the criteria by which teachers' effectiveness should be judged, therefore, is a crucial one. Typically those passing an opinion on teachers' classroom competence will look at one or more of three aspects:

- *The behaviour and experiences of pupils* (whether what they are doing is worthwhile, whether they appear to be absorbed in their task or are misbehaving, the extent to which the task matches the pupils' ability and previous experiences).
- *The behaviour of the teacher* (professional skills such as the ability to explain new concepts, ask appropriate questions, manage the badly behaved, prepare lessons, organise a classroom, assess and monitor progress).
- *Outcomes of teaching* (what pupils appear to have learned, including the knowledge, skills, attitudes and values they acquire as a direct or indirect result of whatever the teacher has done).

I shall be returning to the question of what teachers and children do in the classroom in Part 2, but the matter of outcomes is an important one. The issue of short-term and long-term objectives has already been mentioned and this raises a number of further questions about the basis for any appraisal of teachers' competence.

In Croydon a firm of management consultants was brought in to scrutinise the efficiency and effectiveness of schools. Efficiency was defined as how well each school used its resources, and effectiveness as the extent to which stated and agreed objectives were actually being achieved, which begs the question as to whether they were worthwhile in the first place. One end result was that schools in similar circumstances were linked and then given an efficiency factor relative to each other. Thus if school A obtained 100 and school B 65, then the second school appeared to be significantly less efficient than the first.

It is but a small step to apply the same notion to teachers. If the teacher of class A obtains a factor of 100 based on test scores and the teacher or arguably similar class B a factor of 65, then this looks like a distinctly negative appraisal for the second teacher. The central approach, based as it is on the industrial input–output model, is flawed.

It is certainly sound practice to avoid comparisons between teachers based on raw scores. There is some interesting work at Sheffield University, directed by Dr John Gray, showing that social class is by far the most powerful predictor of GCE and CSE results, much more so than teaching skill. Any comparison of raw unadjusted test or public examination scores as a criterion measure of a teacher's competence would, therefore, be extremely unfair, and teachers of remedial classes would inevitably appear to be less competent than their colleagues who taught abler and more privileged children. Consequently, either various statistical techniques, such as multiple regression analysis or analysis of covariance, have been used to adjust test scores to compensate for initial differences in classes, or schools or classes have been matched in some way. The weakness of both approaches is, first that there is no agreement amongst statisticians about how to eliminate pre-existing differences between unequal groups, and second that matching classes is not as easy as it sounds. Most teachers can recall teaching classes that were thought to be of parallel ability within a school or from year to year, but which turned out to be quite different in reality.

There are other factors which need to be borne in mind when test scores are contemplated as a criterion measure of effective teaching. Take the appraisal of a teacher's work in the field of health education as an example. It would be easy to give a test purely on *knowledge* and judge the effectiveness of the teaching solely on that: do children know what plaque is, can they describe the effects of heavy smoking? But much of this knowledge might only be valuable as a beginning. Tests of the recall of factual information may tell us little about *understanding* (do the children actually understand the link between diet or exercise and good health?), *skills* (can they clean their teeth using the sort of brush and movement which will reduce the likelihood of decay?), *attitudes* (children can be knowledgeable about the need for a balanced diet but have a negative attitude to anything other than junk food and chips), and *behaviour* (they may know all about the connection between smoking and lung and cardiovascular disease, but still smoke heavily). Tests of factual knowledge have an important place in education, but they certainly do not tell the whole story.

A further point to be considered is the extent to which, if judged substantially by test scores, teachers will tend to teach narrowly, concentrating on coaching for the next assessment. In the United States the notion of performance-contracting, the process whereby private firms were hired to teach children to read because teachers were thought to be failing, fell into disrepute when it was discovered that some of the more shady operators were simply rehearsing the test questions.

On the other hand there is some advantage to using tests judiciously. All of us who work in teaching are prone to delude ourselves about what our classes have learned from us. Good diagnostic tests, either purchased from outside or devised within the school, can help review the past and point out what needs to be done in the future. I should sooner see a primary school Head and class teacher jointly reviewing the results of an appropriate diagnostic reading test as part of an appraisal which would cover the efforts of both of them as members of a school staff, than have the

Head give the teacher a wigging because scores on an achievement test are a bit down on last year.

In summary, pupil tests can be a part of the appraisal process, but the following points should be respected:

- Tests of short-term memory may ignore longer-term objectives.
- Unadjusted test scores may merely favour teachers of more able children and disfavour those of less able classes rather than reflect teaching skill.
- Tests requiring the recall of factual information may ignore such factors as understanding, the acquisition of skills, and changes in attitude or behaviour.
- The consequences of over-emphasising test scores may be to narrow the curriculum to those aspects which are to be tested.
- The use of diagnostic tests, either externally produced or devised by teachers themselves, which reveal pupils' strengths and weaknesses in a field, might be more useful as part of the whole school appraisal process than retrospective achievement tests alone.

One useful activity set out in Activity Box 2 can help a group try to elicit its own criteria of effectiveness by thinking of effective and ineffective teachers each member has had, and then pooling experiences to elicit similarities and differences. Some of these points will recur when classroom observation is discussed in Section 2 and under the heading of pupils' views of teaching on page 52. Most participants enjoy the exercise and anyone claiming not to be able to remember a good or bad teacher should be chided. Even people in their 70s and 80s can often recall vividly, albeit with some occasional distortions, the people who taught them. It is especially important for teachers taking part to think of people who taught them, rather than professional colleagues. It is the child's perspective which is important here.

Activity 2 **What is good teaching?**

Aim The purpose of the session is to allow people in the group to analyse effective teaching by pooling their own experiences.

Timing About 5 minutes to set up, 10–15 minutes to do and 40–45 minutes of discussion. About an hour altogether.

Task 1. Explain that each member of the group must think of two teachers he or she had at school, one who was particularly good

and one who was especially poor. They should preferably, but not exclusively, be people who taught them during the same phase of education, primary, secondary or beyond, as the school or college with which the group is concerned.
2. Allow about 15 minutes for people to make rough notes under the headings 'Teacher A' (good), 'Teacher B' (poor). About half way through (7 or 8 minutes) remind people to move on to Teacher B. The chairman should join in and complete the task along with the others.
3. A useful tip, which the chairman can feed in at the beginning, is that if people find it a little difficult to make notes it sometimes helps if they recall specific events (a confrontation, a kind word, a piece of unfairness, a piece of encouragement) which were illustrative of the teacher's effectiveness or lack of it.

Discussion
1. Ask a number of people to describe *briefly* their 'good' teacher (Teacher A). There is no need for every single member of the group to have a turn, and indeed it would become tedious if all participants spoke one after another.
2. Move on to ask people to describe their 'bad' teacher (Teacher B).

Conclusion
1. See if any common features emerge. For example, how many members of the group chose to specialise subsequently in the subject taught by Teacher A or to teach in that age range because of his/her influence? Did children generally appear to dislike Teacher B?
2. Are there contradictions? For example, did some 'good' teachers appear to be well prepared and other 'good' teachers not?
3. Were the 'bad' teachers the exact opposite of the 'good' teachers, or were there attributes shown by both good and bad?
4. What appear to be the group's criteria of effective teaching?
enthusiasm?
warmth?
businesslike organisation?
good discipline?
fairness?
interest in pupils as individuals?
ability in their subject?
or were Teachers A and B selected by members so disparate and unique that no clear patterns of effectiveness can be elicited?
5. How might what has emerged from this session influence the school's appraisal procedures?

Appraisal within the context of school organisation

Since the Second World War there have been significant re-organisations of both primary and middle schools. The drive by all governments from 1950 to the late 1970s to reduce class sizes, extend the school leaving age and improve pupil–teacher ratios led to a doubling in size of the teaching force in a relatively short period of time. In England and Wales the number increased from 200,000 in the early 1950s to about 480,000 by the late 1970s. Around 1970 there were over 100,000 students training to be teachers, but the impact of falling pupil enrolments reduced this to some 30,000 by the mid 1980s. In Scotland in 1979 one third of primary teachers were in their twenties. By 1984 this had fallen to one fifth.

The result of this rising and then falling graph of recruitment is that the teaching profession is ageing in schools, colleges and higher education. By the early 1990s near enough two thirds of all teachers will be over the age of forty. Thus teacher appraisal is introduced to a mature rather than novice profession. Had mandatory appraisal been brought in during the late 1960s or early 1970s, schools would have been bulging with probationers or young teachers in their twenties, fresh from initial training and the experience of being observed and assessed by their supervising tutors and teachers.

Recognising the increasing maturity of the profession many schools, both primary and secondary, have tried to minimise the distance between senior and junior teachers. The structure is often akin to that of a cottage loaf (and this is no reflection on the shape of many teachers over forty) with a senior management group consisting of Head, deputies and scaled post holders in primary schools, or heads of departments and year groups in secondary schools and a large group of basic scale teachers. The structural shape of many organisations which already have a formal system of appraisal, such as the Police, the Armed Forces, the BBC, the Civil Service and numerous businesses, is more clearly hierarchical, often a tall thin triangle with a considerable distance between top and bottom and numerous ranks in between.

The clearly superior–subordinate style of appraisal worked out in some hierarchies might not suit as well a school structure where the emphasis was more on collegiality than rank or status. In small primary schools an especially formal style of appraisal might actually change professional relationships in a way that would benefit nobody. The introduction of a greater degree of formality is inescapable if schools which have never had a regular system of appraisal introduce one for the first time. The real question is: how much of a shock to the system will it be in the first instance? Hence the value of extensive discussions and the involvement of staff at all levels. Anything seen purely as an imposition from some distant senior management team operating a stratosphere away from the rough and tumble of daily classroom life would inevitably encounter resistance.

This raises fundamental questions about appraisal: who should do it, and how might it be undertaken? Both of these issues will be dealt with more fully in Section 2 which covers in more detail the various approaches which might be employed.

Peer appraisal For two people of equal rank*, say two basic scale teachers, two deputy heads, two heads of department, to appraise each other, is seen as a soft option by many people. It is believed that they will simply confirm each other's practices, engage in mutual congratulation and then go on happily about their business without breaking their stride. Badly done, of course, complacency would be reinforced, especially if two teachers who had little or no experience of other schools were either too easily satisfied or too embarrassed to offer anything other than soothing remarks. During the DES-funded Teacher Education Project, however, which I directed with Clive Sutton at the Universities of Nottingham, Leicester and Exeter, we did a great deal of work with pairs of both beginners and experienced teachers.

The evaluations of this work were extremely positive, even at deputy head level, where many deputies reported that being paired with a fellow deputy at another school and visiting each other, studying one another's job and interviewing the Head and staff of the other deputy's school was one of the most interesting and valuable professional activities they had ever undertaken. What was essential for all levels, however, from beginner to experienced senior teacher, was the provision of some degree of *structure* and there will be more about this in Section 2. The Teacher Education Project team was able to provide a written format within which reciprocal pairs could work, and having a focus and shape to the activity helped prevent it degenerating into formless waffle. Peer appraisal, therefore, can both be valuable and have an effect on practice. My personal view is that, skilfully handled and with the right type and amount of supporting structure, it can make more inroads into improving classroom teaching than many other forms of practice.

Superior-subordinate appraisal The most logical structure for appraisal in hierarchical organisations is for each person in the

---

*Two people of *unequal* rank can also work this way. Indeed, in order to minimise the sense of hierarchy, some senior teachers, Heads and deputies in both primary and secondary schools would want to work alongside their colleagues in a classroom, each appraising the work of the other. In this guide, therefore, the term 'peer appraisal' includes people of unequal rank working together as if they are of equal rank.

pyramid to be appraised by the person on the rank immediately above. In schools this would mean that teachers on the basic professional scale would be appraised by Heads, deputies or holders of special responsibility payments in primary schools and by their head of department in secondary schools. In turn the middle managers would be appraised by the Heads who would be scrutinised by the local authority advisers or inspectors, themselves the subject of review by the chief adviser who would be appraised by the senior officers such as the Chief Education Officer or Director of Education. Beyond this presumably the Queen, the Pope and the Prime Minister would be drafted in. The weakness of this process is that at certain stages the superior may not have the specialist knowledge. Secondary heads of departments should be *au fait* with matters in their own subject, but a deputy head who is a mathematician may be lost within a modern language department, and a Chief Adviser may not understand the job of, say, a PE adviser.

All this assumes that superior–subordinate appraisal can only work in one direction, from the top down. There is no reason, however, why subordinate–superior appraisal cannot take place. Senior people would be well advised, during appraisal interviews, to build in questions about themselves, especially about how well, in the eyes of the respondent, they are doing their own job, and what suggestions there might be for improving how the school or the department is run. The need for an agreed structure is just as pressing as it is for peer appraisal.

Needless to say, staffroom criticisms of the Head, or advisers' scathing comments in the County Hall bar about the Chief Education Officer may not be readily forthcoming when the parties are actually face to face, and the courage expressed confidently to colleagues the night before quickly evaporates or turns into bootlicking. Nevertheless a genuinely reciprocated exchange of views ought to be possible.

In my own department at Exeter University the Professors from time to time hold such interviews with our large lecturing staff. On one occasion I asked a colleague during the interview if there was any criticism he would like to make of myself as head of department or about the running of the School of Education. 'Yes,' he replied, 'I meant to tell you this at the time but I never got round to it. You fixed a meeting with a group of my students to talk about their views of their course and you never told me about it and I think you should have done.' Now this was someone I had seen every day, spoken with on numerous occasions and with whom I got on well. The course had been a new one and I had mentioned to him at the beginning of the session that I would talk to the students towards the end of the year to see how they felt it had gone. Unfortunately, I had not thought to tell him of it several months later when I actually met them. He was clearly upset by this. I was able to apologise and learn something, and the whole affair might have rankled indefinitely had I not on this slightly ritualised occasion actually asked outright for his comments. We can too easily delude ourselves that because we meet daily there are no misunderstandings or ways of improving what we do that are not discussed as a matter of course.

Outsider appraisal In order to give a broader perspective, it is often argued that outsiders must be brought in, otherwise fresh practices will never be introduced following an appraisal exercise. Should an outsider element be contemplated there are several possibilities. The first is that of the insider/outsider, that is teachers and Heads from one school being released on occasions to join an appraisal exercise in another school, though this has time and money cost implications which will be discussed again in Section 3. The process will already be familiar to teachers who have been engaged in cross-moderation for Mode 3 public examinations. The advantage of the insider/outsider is that it is someone who is actually doing a similar job but in a different environment. A particularly bold experiment would be to pair teachers in different schools systematically for mutual appraisal; the cross-fertilisation of numerous such 'pen friends' could be extremely valuable for all concerned.

A second possibility is to use local authority inspectors and advisers, who are in any case extensively involved in seeing lessons and counselling teachers and Heads. At the present levels of staffing in most local authorities, however, they would not be able to cover the several thousands of teachers in their area, especially in the primary field which is usually very much understaffed for the large number of small scattered schools one finds in many parts of the country. Probably advisers can best be used for the appraisal of Heads and senior staff, possibly for heads of departments, for probationers with whom they tend to be involved already, and for teachers whose work is unsatisfactory.

A third outsider option is to hire a group of people specially for the assignment of appraising teachers. Other countries have such figures, sometimes known as 'evaluators', usually deeply hated by teachers who see them as bureaucrats or parasites. However much teachers dislike Heads or LEA advisers at least they recognise that they have a job to do. State or regional inspectors who only exist to give grades are viewed with deep suspicion and mistrust. In France, for example, both the Head and an Academy Inspector award an annual mark, the Inspector's grade being based on the observation of a single lesson and a short subsequent conversation. The teacher may or may not be notified in advance of the Inspector's visit. In West Germany, where teachers are civil servants and where there is some variety in the various Länder, a report on each teacher is usually drawn up by the Head and Inspectors frequently countersign these without further ado. Since West Germany has had a very similar pattern of births to Britain during the last thirty years, Inspectors have tended to concentrate on the problems of falling pupil numbers and redeployment. They tend, therefore, to see only the best and poorest teachers or those being moved to another school. Experience elsewhere suggests that the total outsider who has no involvement with a school or individual teacher other than a rare visit to see and grade a lesson may have a limited, if any, part to play in British schools. Her Majesty's Inspectorate plays a quite different role which does involve extensive observation of lessons and evaluation of schools, but does not include detailed written and graded appraisals of individual teachers being put into their personal files with direct promotion or career implications.

Appraisal by lay people Appraisal of teachers by anyone other than educational professionals is a contentious matter. It would be theoretically possible for pupils, parents, governors or ratepayers generally to have a say, but there is no real tradition of their being involved through their elected political representatives on councils and education committees. Elected politicians are quite rightly involved in decisions about education and are frequently members of governing bodies and therefore of selection committees, but

'So much for the External Evaluator.'

judging the worth of individual teachers in their classrooms and schools is a different matter.

It is again a question of personal taste, but I think there would also be some unease about lay governors and parents being *directly* involved in appraisal. This is not, however, to rule out *indirect* involvement. If, for example, parents have regularly complained to the Head about a teacher's failure to set and mark homework, arrive punctually, or inability to be fair in the use of rewards and punishments, then this information should have been brought to the attention of the teacher concerned as appropriate, and ought to be part of any appraisal interview if it has been a regular occurrence with little or no response from the teacher concerned. Equally, on the many occasions when parents comment favourably on teachers' care and concern, skill at bringing out the best in their child or contribution to extra-curricular clubs and societies, visits or field trips, this too should form part of the recognition of a teacher's positive contribution to the school. When it comes to a more formal stocktaking the main difficulty about parents' views is that they are second-hand and that some children do not communicate well about what has happened in school.

In the case of appraisal by pupils much will depend on their age and the disposition of their teachers towards feedback from the front-line consumers of education. Evaluative questionnaires, staff – student committees and end-of-year discussions about courses are not unknown in higher education but have been less frequent in schools. In the United States there have been examples of student ratings forming the basis for lecturers' merit awards. Some academic staff tried to curry favour by awarding generous marks to their classes, but in general this was usually spotted by the students who frequently made scathing references to the practice in their evaluations.

The significant factor about pupils' views of teachers and teaching is that there is a remarkable consistency about them. Kurt Lewin, the American social psychologist, believed that children as young as three or four could be more sensitive than we might suspect to the teaching skill or lack of it of adults with whom they had contact. The research literature on pupils' opinions of teachers and teaching has frequently provided a similar or the same set of precepts. While adults argue about effective teaching, pupils regularly say they prefer teachers who:

- Are slightly firm (rather than permissive or very strict).
- Explain things clearly.
- Show fairness in general and in their use of rewards and punishments.

- Have a sense of humour (though children dislike sarcasm).
- Are enthusiastic and stimulating rather than dull and boring.
- Show interest in them as individuals.

In one form or another these characteristics come up with children of different ages and in various types of school.

Furthermore, there can be considerable agreement amongst pupils about individual teachers. I once used a behavioural checklist with items such as 'This teacher is usually interested in our answers' to elicit the views of 1000 children in nearly 40 classrooms. It was notable that on most items a class would divide 25 Yes 5 No or 3 Yes 27 No rather than 50/50. In the Teacher Education Project (Wragg, 1984) we found that, in interview, groups of pupils would in general show high agreement about their various teachers' skills and attributes.

If pupils are able to give consistent and reliable information why are they not consulted more frequently? Most teachers would be very concerned if pupil ratings or comments formed a central part of their formal appraisal, and therefore affected directly their career prospects, but I shall be discussing in Section 2 how pupils' views might be noted in a less threatening but possibly more effective way.

Self-appraisal If teachers are to improve what they do as a result of any appraisal system they must change their behaviour in some way. Whatever power-coercive methods are used, ultimately teachers must make their own decision to do things differently. Self-appraisal has an important part to play, therefore, and some would argue it is even more important than analysis by others. Indeed, before teacher appraisal became a political and legal matter there was quite a positive development in many schools and local authorities of self-appraisal schemes where individual teachers, departments, and the whole school took stock of what they were trying to accomplish and how effectively they were achieving their objectives.

Most frequently these, often local authority sponsored schemes, used written self-reports or responses to checklists at teacher level to collect information, with procedures often worked out by groups of Heads, teachers and administrators. Occasionally the sheer size of what teachers were asked to scrutinise could become too formidable. It is one thing to undertake a bout of soul-searching as a group, quite another to flagellate oneself with an overwhelming checklist in one's own attic late at night. Nonetheless, given group support and a manageable task, the careful private sorting out of what one is doing is worthwhile and will be taken up again later.

Closed or open appraisal?

The arguments about open and closed reporting systems have been well rehearsed. In general they include the following points.

Closed appraisal The people being appraised do not see any written report or grade and are not made fully aware of any adverse criticisms of them, though they may be given a verbal overview of the general tone of a report. Supporters of a closed reporting system argue that it allows those conducting a review to be frank and honest, to pull no punches, rather than be mealy-mouthed and diplomatic. Another point often advanced is that teachers could easily be demoralised if confronted with too blunt an appraisal, especially as the job is so demanding that all who practise it are bound to fall short of what they and others would like to achieve.

Open appraisal The people being appraised see the report written about them. The chief arguments in favour of the open reporting system are that people fantasise about reports they have not seen, often imagining put-downs where none exist; that those in positions of authority acquire even more unchecked power if they can write secret reports; that the information recorded may be inaccurate and so the subject of the report should be allowed to check it or comment on it; that part of the value of an appraisal is that it can be discussed openly with a view to improving future practice; and that, especially with a mature teaching profession, an open system encourages trust and mutual respect. In many cases where open reports are written the subject is asked to sign a statement which says something like, 'I have read this report and checked and discussed its contents'. Sometimes there is a further space for the respondent to comment or record any disagreements or explanation.

The question of open or closed reports must be discussed early in the process of establishing an appraisal system, as must the related matters of the form of any written paper and the 'ownership' of it. There has already been considerable discussion about whether a written appraisal 'belongs' to the teacher, the school or the local authority. Some of these matters will be resolved outside the context of the individual school, often between local authorities and teacher unions, but where there is doubt, latitude for interpretation or no agreed procedure, all parties need to know where they stand before the process begins, because such matters will affect not only people's perceptions of it but also their response to it.

My own view on this particular matter is very clear: I should prefer an open system with teachers or others being appraised able to read, countersign and add comments to any written report; teachers should have their own copy, the original should be kept in the school, and local authority advisers and officers should have access to it provided the teacher is told when and why it has been consulted.

Part 2 Methods of appraisal

I was sitting in a radio studio waiting to talk about teacher appraisal when the producer came in and said he would first play over the tape of an actual appraisal interview, recorded in a school which was already engaged in the exercise, so that I could hear the part of the programme immediately preceding my own contribution. I listened with growing unease as an extremely pleasant-sounding Head held a soothing conversation with an equally pleasant teacher, the gist of which seemed to be, 'Keep up the good work with the cubs and try to find time to finish off that enquiry into what the parents think of us, and all will be well'. Inevitably the stage-managed role-play for the benefit of radio will only be an approximation to the real thing, but I was left with an awful feeling that the whole endeavour might easily revolve around interesting but safe matters, rather than the professional realities of classroom life. I propose to devote much of this section to the analysis, observation and improvement of classroom practice, not because this ought to be the sole focus of appraisal, but because it should, in my view, be right at the centre.

There are several options open to participants in the appraisal process, and though techniques in themselves achieve little unless they are implemented skilfully, it is important that many possibilities are explored and considered. Classroom observation can have a valuable place in that teachers enjoy discussing their work with someone who understands what it involves. The observation of lessons provides plenty of talking points, but it is not the only way to raise matters about teaching and learning. In the training of social workers, for example, it may not be desirable to have two people present with a 'client', so the trainee may be asked to recreate a session, to describe it or write an account of it, for the supervisor to be able to suggest strategies or comment on actual processes. The same procedure can be used for teaching if necessary, though my own preference would still be for direct observation.

An appraisal interview can also be a valuable event, and decisions have to be made about how formal or informal it should be, the degree of structure, who might be involved, and what might follow it. Some teachers quite like using questionnaires or checklists for self-analysis, or pupil feedback, and these too will be considered. With the spread of modern technology, most schools have a light portable cassette recorder, and several own or have access to a video recorder. There are problems recording in classrooms, which usually have a substantial amount of background noise, such as chairs scraping on uncarpeted floors, but these are not insuperable. Certainly there is no shortage of methods of implementing teacher appraisal, though each of them will depend on the skill and sensitivity of those applying them, none being idiot-proof.

Classroom observation

Most teachers would hate to be evaluated by hearsay alone. If they were told that they were to receive a negative evaluation because of some overheard piece of gossip, or because another person had reported that their class had seemed a little noisy one day the previous week, they would be extremely upset. 'But you've never seen me teach', would be the obvious response, 'why don't you come and see what I actually do, instead of relying on guesswork and rumour?' Yet because there has been no strong tradition in Britain of teachers being watched in their classroom on a regular basis, it is well known that they and their class may well behave differently if an adult observer is present.

In many schools in the United States, the Principal, Vice Principal and several other senior staff give a considerable amount of time to lesson observation and discussion. One New York High School Principal told me that it was the most important contribution he thought he could make to his school, because in staff discussion about curriculum, teaching methods or the quality of pupils' work, he could offer the benefit of first-hand experience from hundreds of lessons which gave him an overview of what was going on in the school. In another Junior High School I visited in Connecticut, pupils were used to other teachers being present for observation, and it was not uncommon for a video camera to be sited in the corner of a room when teachers wished to record and play back any of their lessons. As a result there was no commotion and little surprise when someone other than the teacher walked in and sat at the back of a classroom.

The role and effect of the observer

Curious to know what effect an observer might have on classroom behaviour one investigator (Samph, 1976) installed microphones in classrooms and then sent in observers, either announced or unexpected, some weeks later. He discovered that, when observed, teachers tended to ask a large number of questions, use more praise and make greater play with pupils' answers than when no one else was present. Observers' status and reputation may have a noticeable effect on a class. A senior teacher, who has a reputation as a strict disciplinarian, can sit in on the lessons of a student teacher experiencing problems of class control, and the student will find that pupils simply get on with their work for once. Teachers can react to visitors by second-guessing what prejudices and beliefs the observer has and then trying to provide a model which will elicit approval, or obversely by being independent and doing whatever they would have done had no one appeared. Some will simply behave in a more pupil-centred way than usual, as in the Samph study, and others may feel more obliged to 'perform' so that their skills are on public display.

Observers, too, need to be aware of the effects of their own presence, as well as of certain peculiarities common to the process. There are two phenomena in particular that must be recognised. The first is that of *projection*. The observer imagines himself actually teaching the class, and thinks more in terms of what he would do in the circumstances, rather than of the teacher being witnessed. The danger here is that instead of the modestly competent practitioner he might be, the observer projects himself as a paragon: the lesson would not be allowed to flag, that child at the back would be spotted misbehaving and be told off in a firm but, of course, kindly manner, and the class as a whole would be exceptionally busy and hang on every word of his own explanation, story-telling or questioning. The art of constructive observation is to wrench oneself away from these fantasies and concentrate on helping the teacher.

The second potential problem is that of *compensation*; that is, the tendency to seek to make up for one's own deficiencies. Thus the observer who is untidy or badly organised may be excessively punitive over this characteristic in others. When the observer's own failings are well known to the person being observed this form of hypocrisy is not only irritating but makes legitimate comments incredible. A student teacher once remarked about his tutor, 'He keeps going on about my visual aids being inadequate as if he's obsessed with it, but I can't ever remember him using a single visual aid in any of his sessions with us'. A more acceptable approach is occasionally to say something like, 'As one who is not always the world's best organised person myself I have seen the problems this can cause me, so I want to make sure you don't get caught in the same traps'.

The power relationship between observer and observed is also relevant. A powerful Head of a large secondary school may reduce a newly arrived probationer to a nervous jelly, not because of any particular act but simply because of the huge gap in status. Many people of high status are adept at recognising this potential problem and defusing it, some seem oblivious or even exacerbate it by entering the room with a big presence, bristling with briefcase, pens and clipboard, or even taking over the lesson at some stage. Observers should also be aware of factors such as sex or ethnic group, in that some teachers find it more of a strain to be watched by a person of the opposite sex, for example. Nonetheless, classroom observation, despite the initial difficulties and apprehensions it may cause, is well worthwhile, and it is important in schools which wish to make use of it, first of all that the necessary time should be found, because it is a most labour-intensive activity, and secondly that it becomes so commonplace and taken for granted that teachers and pupils behave as naturally as possible when it occurs.

What to focus on in the classroom observation

There has been a considerable growth in interest in the study of classroom processes since the 1960s, and there are now thousands of published studies. Some investigators prefer to use a set of predetermined categories, others opt for the more open-ended style of the social anthropologist who keeps books of field notes. I have summarised these various approaches and listed some of the

'Entering the room with a big presence.'

numerous books now available in *Classroom Teaching Skills* (Wragg, 1984). The first question the observer needs to ask is the particular purpose of any visit to a classroom. If a person is known to be an excellent all-round class teacher, say, in a primary school which is anxious to improve its work in science and technology, then the purpose of observing her and the methods adopted might be quite different from a case where someone is experiencing discipline problems or about whom there have been complaints.

The use of categories There is now quite a long tradition of using some sort of schedule when watching a lesson, which involves categories or sub-headings. These might be broad, like 'class management', or more specific such as 'teacher asks question requiring the recall of factual information'. A distinction is often drawn between *low* and *high inference* categories. In the former the observer notes the occurrence of discrete events requiring relatively little personal judgement; in the latter much more analysis and evaluation is required.

Imagine a situation where you have to visit a classroom because the local health specialists have announced they wish to reduce the spread of infectious and contagious diseases. Your task is to see how healthy or unhealthy each classroom seems. A high inference response would be to ask you to report under such headings as 'hygiene' or 'awareness of health risks'; a low inference approach would identify pieces of behaviour said by doctors to be related to some degree of risk of infection, and ask you to observe the frequency of occurrences by noting events such as 'child sneezes without use of a handkerchief', 'child washes hands after using toilet', or 'child coughs without covering mouth'. Both styles of category have their uses and the situation should determine which one, or what mixture, makes most sense.

Early classroom interaction studies concentrated almost entirely on the teacher, but recently there has been more interest in looking at pupils. Some schedules use a mixture of categories or headings which bring in both teachers and pupils. It would be easy to focus entirely on what teachers do, over-emphasising the performance aspect again, and lose sight of pupils' responses or initiations.

In devising sub-headings and categories, observers need to be aware of the many pitfalls. Here are two checklist items with problems attached:

- *'Teacher fails to praise pupil'*. It is usually better to concentrate on what teachers actually do rather than what they do not do, though this kind of observation put in context in a notebook rather than in a predetermined schedule might be of interest.

- *'Child shows interest and asks teacher a question'*. This requires the observer to look for two events, showing interest and asking a question, which might not be linked or might occur separately.

Observers will need to decide at what level of detail they seek to record events. The potential range is enormous and there are hundreds of published schedules which have been used in research or curriculum development projects, or devised as part of some initial or in-service training programme. Most are not especially well-suited for teacher appraisal. Many research instruments operate at too minute a level of detail. If one thinks of a very simple act like writing on the blackboard, a too atomised category approach can make it seem comical: teacher picks up chalk, teacher advances (purposefully/hesitantly) towards blackboard, teacher does/does not trip over podium, teacher drops chalk, child (accidentally/deliberately) treads on chalk; few would want or be able to record all the tiny trivia of commonplace classroom life. In any case such detailed quantitative approaches require a good deal of training, and careful checks on agreement between observers if more than one person is involved. For most teacher appraisal purposes a broader, more generic set of sub-headings may be most suitable. Indeed, there is one very useful exercise a group can undertake at the planning stage based on a videotape or film and this is described in Activity Box 3.

Activity 3	**Classroom observation – what do we look for?**
Purpose	To devise what features of lessons might be most worthy of analysis and discussion with the teacher concerned. About 60–120 minutes will be needed.
Required	A videotape (20–30 minutes) of a lesson as similar as possible to what is typical for the group concerned: for example, a modern language lesson in a secondary school, a project session in a primary school, a lecture/demonstration in further or higher education. It is a good idea to make one's own video in one's own school if possible, or otherwise to borrow one which illustrates a lesson with the same age group or specialist area.
Step 1	The group should watch the video imagining that an interview is to be held with the teacher afterwards in which the observer and teacher will attempt to analyse and improve classroom practice. Each person should make notes during the video about *what aspects* of the lesson might be discussed.

Step 2 The group compares notes, and tries to see if certain *headings* suggest themselves: for example, 'preparation and planning', 'class management', 'teachers' questions', 'pupil participation', 'personal relationships', etc.

Step 3 There should be a consideration of other possible topics of conversation not suggested in this lesson. For example, the lesson might have involved, on this particular occasion, no practical, small group or project work which might legitimately be a feature of other lessons. The list of headings under Step 2, therefore, should be broadened to include such other possibilities. Furthermore, the group needs to be aware that its horizons may be too limited by current practice so imagination must be used to widen the possible scope.

Step 4 A sample proforma covering no more than two sides of A4 paper should be drawn up. If the group is large it is often best to break up into smaller groups of no more than four people for this phase. The proforma should show the main and subsidiary headings and layout of a recording sheet on which an observer might make notes.

Step 5 Usually the group will have generated quite a deal of energy and talk by now, so it is often best to photocopy each sub-group's proforma and distribute the full set to members for further discussion and action at a future meeting. The use of outsiders is valuable here to give a fresh perspective. There would be advantage in two schools working together and/or exchanging findings.

Footnote There is one delicate matter to be considered if the teacher shown on videotape is also a member of the group doing Activity 3, which may be the case. The purpose of this activity is not to demolish people who have been brave enough to put their own lesson up for public viewing, but rather to focus on what aspects of teaching seem to be worth developing. It may sometimes be better, therefore, if a stranger's lesson is used, or, alternatively, if it is made clear to the whole group that this colleague's teaching is merely a vehicle for lubricating discussion and planning, not an excuse either to tear the poor devil to shreds or to elicit an embarrassing volume of compliments.

There are many possible shapes to any lesson observation schedule and the following are amongst the key sub-headings which frequently occur.

Preparation and planning Experienced teachers vary in the way they undertake their planning, some keeping extensive written notes, others holding much of it in their heads. An observer might note the extent to which what is seen appears to be part of a plan. Discussion might centre on the teacher's short-term and longer-term intentions and the extent to which careful and coherent planning, or the lack of it, seems apparent in the lessons observed.

Teachers' questions   Some studies have shown teachers asking on average 350 questions a day, and this rate might be higher at times when rapid question and answer is an integral part of teaching and learning. The evidence also suggests that roughly three out of every five questions require the recall of factual information ('What is the capital of France?'), one out of five involves the management of the class ('Have you all got your books?') and one out of five is what some people call 'higher order' questions, that is those requiring evaluation, analysis, imagination, more than simple recall ('Did the United Nations do a good job during the Falklands War?', 'What might have happened if the Spanish Armada had won?'). Sometimes a distinction is made between questions which are 'closed' where the answer is a known textbook one, or 'open' where several responses are possible.

So far as appraisal is concerned there is no 'right' kind of question. Some quantified studies have sought to establish a link between the frequency of asking questions and pupils' learning, but no firm linear relationship of this kind has emerged. What seems to be more important is judging when it is appropriate to ask what kind of question. In a research project looking at professional skills which I once directed, the teacher who obtained the highest test scores from 8 and 9-year-old pupils after teaching the topic 'Insects' was one who began his lesson by asking, 'Is a bird and insect?'. After a scornful dismissal of this apparently foolish question by the class, pupils were pressed to say why it was not. Gradually all the characteristics of insects' body shape, wings, legs and so on were elicited. Had he asked twenty or thirty such questions he might have confused his class. On this occasion one well-chosen and pursued key question seemed sufficient.

It would make sense, therefore, for an observer to consider such aspects of questioning as:

- *Appropriateness* Does the teacher use questions suitable for the whole class or for the individuals concerned? Is the language choice right for the age and ability of the children? Is it relevant to the topic being learned?
- *Variety* Does the teacher vary questions or are they always of the same kind? Are they always addressed to or answered by the same pupils? (Some research has shown that most questions are

answered by pupils sitting in a V-shaped wedge in front of the teacher).
- *Pupil responses* Are these short or long? How does the teacher react to answers? With interest? enjoyment? boredom? indifference? praise? criticism? Do the pupils' answers suggest they understand the question? Does the teacher ever build on pupils' responses?
- *Sequences* Does the teacher's line of questioning cohere? Or is it more random and haphazard? Does the teacher probe further after an initial thought-provoking question?

Explaining Of the many presentation skills that teachers develop, the ability to explain clearly and the strategies teachers use to elicit understanding are most appreciated by pupils, as was pointed out above. There are critical moments in pupils' learning when a clear explanation of a new concept, of a child's problem or difficulty, or of the relationship between what has been learned previously and what is being studied now, is absolutely crucial either at whole class or individual pupil level. Teachers may well invest five or six minutes at the beginning of a one-hour block, half or whole day or longer, in explaining what the class will do or motivating and enthusing them to pursue their individual or group project. Well conducted it will lubricate the rest of the session, badly done it could kill all interest and understanding.

Many children reach a plateau from time to time, or arrive at a particular point where proper understanding is critical. It is here that clear and comprehensible explanations are especially vital. Take the following common examples:

- A pupil encounters algebra for the first time and has to understand the use of letters instead of numbers.
- A science class meets the term 'inversely proportional' in a Physics law (difficult and off-putting on the surface, but the notion, with hand signals, that 'the more you have of this, the less you have of that', is not especially perplexing).
- A child starts school needing to learn the school and classroom rules and conventions.
- A PE class is introduced to the game of basketball.

In each case skilful or unskilful communication by the teacher may determine whether someone is successful at mathematics or physics or switches off, enjoys or hates starting school, or participates in or rejects sport.

It is not essential for every 'explanation' to consist of a diatribe from the teacher. Many will unlock understanding by setting a piece of practical work, posing questions, demonstrating, and giving or eliciting analogies ('Is this like anything else you have come across?'). A class of 9 and 10 year olds using a microelectronics kit for the first time was a little confused over why inserting a capacitor in their circuit caused a delay in the bulb lighting up, until the teacher pointed out that it was 'like a bucket filling up with water'.

Some of the features mentioned under 'Teachers' questions' above are also worth observers considering here, such as the use of vocabulary and expression appropriate to the individual or class; the clarity of any teacher exposition, both in terms of voice and the making or eliciting of key points essential to understanding; variety of approach including the use of audio or visual aids, practical activities, demonstration by teacher or pupils; the degree and nature of interest and understanding obtained from the children; the use of summaries either given by the teacher or drawn up from the pupils; and the quality of explaining to individuals, small groups or the whole class.

Class management The ability to manage a class underpins many other professional skills which teachers may have. The most knowledgeable people in the world with the most brilliant ability to explain, phrase exactly the right sort of question, prepare interesting-looking lessons, and assess pupils' work, would be lost if they did not exercise control when the need arose, avoid or know how to deal with misbehaviour, organise effectively activities for groups and individuals, and establish good personal relationships and mutual respect. Indeed, inability to control a class is one of the most common reasons for student teachers failing their teaching practice or probationers having their induction period extended. It is also one of the most frequent sources of complaint from parents, and indeed from the pupils who want to learn something but feel their opportunities are diminished by those who disrupt lessons.

It would be wrong, however, for an observer to concentrate exclusively on orderliness. A class can be well behaved but not well managed. Class management also involves the time spent on the task in hand. There is much talk in teaching of pupils' 'motivation' or lack of it. One operational definition of motivation is the amount of time and the degree of arousal or attentiveness which someone brings to an activity. Children who are not motivated will spend little actual time on whatever they are supposed to be doing, preferring instead to stare out of the window, doodle, distract others or chat to their friends.

Time in itself, however, is an empty notion. After all, pupils could be asked to spend a great deal of time on some futile task such as copying out telephone directories. An observer considering teachers' management of children's time in lessons might find helpful the notion of the 'bullseye' which we developed during the Teacher Education Project (Wragg, 1984). In this model a series of concentric circles zooms in from all 168 hours available in a week (circle A), through the time available in school, about 24 hours per week (circle B), to the time actually assigned for some activity, perhaps number work in a primary school or English in a secondary school (circle C). By now we may be down to some three or four hours, and none of the previous circles reflects on the class management skill of the teacher but rather on policy decisions within the local authority and school. However, circle D represents time actually spent on the task in hand, and, since this can vary considerably from class to class and from one individual child to another, the management skill of the teacher does now become influential if not all-determining. Circle E encloses that aspect of the task which is on something arguably worthwhile, which would exclude the copying out of telephone directories, and circle F circumscribes the bullseye, in that children need to obtain a certain amount of success in what they do if they are to learn. Thus the skilful manager of children's time would be one who could maximise the area in the bullseye, that is the amount of time learning something worthwhile with some degree of success.

Incidentally the idea of 'task' is sometimes interpreted too narrowly in this context. I would personally want to include a wide range of worthwhile objectives, including the development of social competence as well as whatever academic purpose is overtly the

Time Circles: a Model of Time Management (not to scale)

Circle A = all time
Circle C = time assigned to a subject
Circle E = time on a worthwhile task

Circle B = time spent in school
Circle D = time actually spent on the task
Circle F = with some degree of success

focus of the activity concerned. In the field of personal, social and moral development, for example, children will learn much in an oblique manner, not solely through the direct medium of lessons entitled PSME. If in a drama class a group is working collaboratively on a project, or in a science lesson three children are conducting and recording an experiment, or in a physical education class pairs or teams are engaged in an activity, a teacher who ensures that pupils help each other, wait their turn, and support rather than denigrate or undermine the group, can be doing valuable work in the field of personal and social development. Given the explosion of knowledge in our society and the importance of knowing how to learn, find out for oneself, work as a member of a collaborating group – all vital for the world of the twenty-first century – certain aspects of process can become as important as content. The broad-minded observer of teachers' class management skills, therefore, will have an eye for the nurturing of curiosity, the development of confidence and the ability to articulate one's point of view, the fostering of sustained application to a task which is proving difficult and which might lead to a loss of interest, along with other parallel concerns to the main objective.

Amongst several sub-headings commonly mentioned under the broad heading of 'class management' are the following – some of which are of central importance, others more peripheral:

- *Preparation* Has the teacher anticipated problems, for example what to do if individuals or groups finish early? Is the activity or set of activities planned likely to engage the interest of the pupils?
- *Beginnings and endings* Does the teacher manage the start and finish of the lesson well? (Entry into the room, setting up the activity, explaining the purpose, clarifying queries or difficulties before pupils start, drawing lesson to a close, tidying away, class leaving room.)
- *Transitions* What happens when there is a change from one type of activity to another, for example when a class splits up into groups after a plenary session, or when the teacher, having told the class a story or held a period of class discussion asks the class to begin writing? (Jacob Kounin, an American researcher, found a higher incidence of indiscipline during transitions.)
- *Movement* How does the teacher handle pupils' movement if and when it occurs? When children move to another position in the room are they orderly or disruptive?
- *Personal relationships* Are relationships between teacher and class good or poor? Teachers who have good relationships tend to have fewer discipline and general management problems than those with poor relationships.
- *Vigilance* Does the teacher appear to have a full picture of what is

happening throughout the whole classroom area? Is there good eye contact with individual pupils? Are pupils' problems, queries or misbehaviour picked up early? Good teachers who are deeply interested in the work of individual children can easily develop tunnel vision and become oblivious to others in the class.
- *Disruptive behaviour* How does the teacher avoid or deal with disruptive behaviour? Is any use of rewards and punishments fair? Is the teacher's response timely, before misbehaviour has escalated, or delayed? Analysis of seriously disruptive incidents has shown that the teacher has in certain cases failed to nip trouble in the bud, and what starts off as innocuous misdemeanour may then escalate.
- *Rules* Are classroom rules, (a) clear, (b) followed? Although some rules on, say, laboratory safety may be explicit and in written form, others may be unwritten or even be local to the individual teacher; for example, no talking when the teacher is addressing the class, pupils must raise their hand to answer and not call out, written work must be set out in a specified form etc. It is these unwritten rules which may be unclear or which may be applied in an inconsistent manner, or lead to confusion and misunderstanding.
- *Pupil involvement* Do pupils generally and individually appear to be interested and involved in what they are doing? Does the teacher include all types of pupil, both boys and girls, more and less able, pupils of different ethnic backgrounds, in such activities as class discussion, demonstrations or the assigning of responsibility?
- *Monitoring of progress* Does the teacher monitor what pupils are doing? When children are working on their own or in groups some teachers fail to check progress and are then disappointed at the poor quality of what has been done. Others may appear to be patrolling the room but are creating a draught rather than actually looking at and discussing pupils' work. On the other hand judging when to intercede and when to allow uninterrupted application to the activity is also an essential part of the teacher's art.
- *Pupil independence* Are pupils able to work independently or are they too dependent on the teacher? One interesting occurrence for observers to contemplate is why the teacher might be penned permanently at a desk behind a long queue of people. Are their questions vital? (for example, explanation of some important new concept) or could they have made their own decisions? (how to spell a word, permission to turn the page).

These are just some of the numerous aspects of class management which an observer might consider. It is important to remember that there are many different ways of handling a class, and that the context is crucial. An incident in one environment might merit a quite different response from a similar event in another. Furthermore class management skill is not necessarily manifested in a high profile, public way in every lesson. During our study of this field in the Teacher Education Project we observed several hundred lessons given by teachers during the first few days of the school year. Many worked hard to establish ways of working which only needed fine tuning thereafter. A visitor later in the school year might have wrongly assumed that certain teachers were simply fortunate to have exceptionally assiduous classes, unaware of the considerable efforts which had gone into the early part of the session. Finally, observers will need to empathise with teachers, especially if they are not themselves involved on a day-to-day basis with a class, and remember that many teachers' decisions about managing a class, handling problems or responding to sudden unruly behaviour, are taken in less than a second. It is often much easier to make the right decision while sitting at the back of a class with a notebook than while actually teaching it.

Observing pupils As the balance in classroom observation has shifted towards what pupils do rather than concentrating solely on a teacher's public 'performance', there has been a development of more methods of studying the behaviour of children in detail. The choices are between trying to observe all pupils as a group or as individuals, or choosing 'target' pupils, perhaps between two and ten, who will be studied as being illustrative of the rest. One commonly used procedure is to find six target pupils, by selecting one boy and one girl amongst high, medium and low ability children in the class. These pupils can then be observed in detail. Another possibility is to choose fewer pupils, perhaps two, who are either a contrast, or who are similar in some way. For example, the observer might study one pupil deeply engaged in the activity and another who appears not to be, or try to find one boy and one girl who took the lead in what their particular group was doing, depending on the particular aims of any observation.

When observing pupils it is easy to be distracted away from any clear purpose. The eye tends to follow attention-catching events: the pupil who walks across the room, the child whose hand goes up to answer a question, the group that starts to giggle at some shared private joke. One useful, though not especially profound way, of avoiding this is to watch every single pupil in the class, one after another, for a fixed period of time, perhaps twenty or thirty seconds each. If necessary a simple sheet can be drawn up like the one below and checks can be made on whether each pupil appears to be manifesting high, medium or low involvement in some legitimate activity related to the lesson, and is behaving well or badly.

INDIVIDUAL PUPIL OBSERVATION SHEET

Class .... Teacher .... Subject .... Date ....

	ON TASK			DEVIANCY		
	LOW	MEDIUM	HIGH	NONE	MILD	MORE SERIOUS
1						
2						
3						
4						
5						
6						
7						
8						
9						
10						
11						
12						
13						
14						
15						
16						
17						
18						
19						
20						
21						
22						
23						
24						
25						
26						
27						
28						
29						
30						
TOTALS						

The value of this kind of exercise is not that it gives a complete account of, say, pupil attentiveness and behaviour, but that the observer does see all kinds of interesting happenings which might otherwise be missed. For example, one sometimes forms the impression that a class is behaving very badly, but scrutiny of every pupil may show that four pupils are responsible for most of the disruptions, that a further three or four occasionally join in, and that twenty others simply get on with their work or sit quietly. It is the children who work steadily who often go unremarked, and looking at each child in turn can force observers to see unspectacular but essential aspects of classroom life which might normally have escaped their attention.

There are some obvious pitfalls in studying pupils. First of all, though it is often very clear it can also be difficult to be sure whether pupils are involved in what is happening or not. Some are adept at feigning being busy, others may give the impression they are doodling or day-dreaming when they are actually planning the next stage of their work. Second, any quantification such as the one on the pupil observation sheet above must be used with great caution. The device is a rough and ready way of measuring, not a precise instrument. It may well give rise to all kinds of interesting conversations with the teacher concerned, but it is not by any means the whole story, and if any observer using it does not feel confident in what has been tallied it should be discarded, though there will still have been some value from the act of perusing the class pupil by pupil.

Matching One especially important aspect of the child's vantage point of classroom life is the notion of matching, which is mentioned frequently in HMI reports both on general matters and on individual schools. It has been discussed especially in the context of primary education, but applies frequently in secondary lessons as well. There are several kinds of matching which need to be considered, the most common of which is the match of the task or activity to the individual child or group.

Neville Bennett (1984) studied the extent to which this match did or did not occur by asking trained observers to interview children about the task in which they were engaged and during the interview to see how well they coped with tasks in a similar field which were either easier or more difficult than the activity in hand. Like HMI he found that able children were frequently being set assignments which were too easy and less able pupils were being asked to undertake activities which were too difficult. The temptation with a class of mixed ability is to pursue the sheepdog tactic of trying to keep people close to the middle of the flock. If teachers do not make a brilliant match on every occasion, however, this is not a matter for blame and punishment, but rather for seeing how a better match can be obtained, given that it is not easy to devise individual assignments, group tasks or options for a class of very varying talents and levels of achievement.

Other aspects of matching include the extent to which the teaching strategies being employed are suitable for the group or individual concerned or indeed to the type of topic or activity being undertaken, for example whether, in a particular science topic, a class needs a lecture, demonstration, practical activity, discussion, or individual worksheet or what combination of these would make best sense.

Subject specialism The discussion above has been about general matters, albeit with some occasional references to particular subjects. There are, however, several matters of particular concern to those observing teachers of specialist subjects, either in the primary or the secondary school. Not the least of these is the quality of the teacher's own knowledge and skill in the relevant subjects. There is no direct linear relationship between how much a teacher knows and teaching skill: in other words, being the world's leading expert in a field is no guarantee that one can communicate with others. There is, however, a threshold effect – too little knowledge at any stage and the teacher will have limited effectiveness. The explosion of knowledge and the development of new skills and techniques is not confined solely to fields such as science, medicine and technology. In every academic discipline the amount of published knowledge has far outstripped the ability of any individual or small team to master more than a tiny fraction of it. The implications for teachers include the following:

- Keeping up to date in what might be not only an expanding but also rapidly changing field.
- Sustaining their own competence in skills as well as knowledge (craft, design and technology is a good example here because of the availability of power tools, fresh processes, and new possibilities such as are offered by developments in microelectronics).
- Having a sufficient overview of the field so that sensible decisions can be made about which topics to teach at what age and ability level.
- Being competent enough in the field to inspire confidence in pupils that the teacher is not permanently dependent on reference books, nor incapable of answering basic questions which are not covered in the textbook or teaching materials.

METHODS OF APPRAISAL

One of the difficulties of observing teachers with a view to appraising the adequacy of their subject knowledge is that this may not always manifest itself. Teachers often steer away from areas where their subject knowledge is thinnest. Although a music teacher who sang out of tune or consistently mangled a piano accompaniment might soon be rumbled, someone who pulled out a tried and tested favourite lesson topic when observed might appear to be well informed.

'I hope you won't take it amiss, Mr Grimsdyke, if I give a non-expert's view on your PE lesson.'

The HMI survey of primary schools, published in 1978, contained a good example of this avoidance of areas where the teacher's knowledge was insecure, when it revealed that only one primary class in ten was enjoying a properly conceived science programme, and that very little physical science was being taught. Few primary teachers at that time had received any significant higher education in the physical sciences, and so tended to opt for nature study topics like tadpoles and sticky buds rather than magnetism or electricity. Important gaps in primary or secondary teachers' specialist knowledge may not become apparent through lesson observation alone and would need to be checked through other means like interview and self-appraisal, both of which are discussed further below.

Another important matter is the many teaching strategies which may be central to one subject or topic but peripheral to another. In science and PE lessons there is a safety dimension which may be less marked in other kinds of activity. Teachers of modern languages may give heed to pronunciation, intonation and fluency, sometimes in a manner unique to their discipline. Science teachers may be using a curriculum package where the emphasis is on pupils being like real scientists and trying to discover scientific laws for themselves from class discussion and experiment. One focus of classroom observation in this context, therefore, might be whether or not the teacher asks questions or sets up conditions which actually encourage pupils to formulate and test their own hypotheses. A Scottish researcher, David Hamilton (1975), found that in integrated science lessons some teachers did the exact opposite of what the curriculum developers had intended, and frustrated pupil enquiry. A primary teacher working with a class on a multi-disciplinary topic will still need special strategies. For example, pupils free to use the library or resources centre as part of their project work will need to learn information-gathering and recording skills, and in any investigation involving fieldwork attention will need to be paid to the sorts of expertise developed by geography or biology fieldworkers or, if interviews are involved, a rudimentary familiarity with the modes of operation employed by social scientists.

Perhaps I can illustrate this specialist angle with some examples from one particular subject area. The examples below are but a tiny sample in no particular order taken from my own notebooks of lesson observations in the field of modern languages, which is a subject in which I happen to have more specialist knowledge than in many other fields. They are in the form of discussion points and suggestions, and they include some of the more critical comments:

- You tended to concentrate almost exclusively on pronunciation and ignore intonation. Children are rehearsing poor intonation patterns.
- When Nigel replied '*das* Wald' you replied 'Ja, *der* Wald'. The class was left uncertain whether it should be *das* or *der*.
- Your use of pairwork to practise the shopping topic was very effective, but some pairs seemed unsure how to use 'acheter' which is a key verb in this context and perhaps needed a special word of explanation first.
- Your own pronunciation of the 'u' sound is faulty and 'tu' comes over consistently as 'chew'. You need to practise this yourself otherwise pupils hear an inadequate model.
- When Alison tried to answer the question about breakfast she got stuck because she did not know the German for 'bacon'. You were managing to sustain some good periods of conversation in the foreign language, but so as not to have avoidable breakdowns it might be useful to teach children to ask you questions like 'Wie sagt man .... auf Deutsch?' or to say 'Ich kenne nicht das Wort ....'
- The notion of the subjunctive as you explained it was too complex for a mixed ability class at this level. Better perhaps to concentrate at this stage on using and understanding one or two common forms like 'ich möchte' or 'ich könnte'.

My notebooks on modern language lessons are also full of complimentary remarks and of general observations about relationships, discipline, visual aids or groupwork, but the point at issue here is that I am unable to give such detailed subject specialist comments about accuracy, alternative possibilities, or the validity of the activity for the age and ability group, in fields where I have less knowledge myself. During an appraisal where the subject specialist elements are important, therefore, it is necessary that the observer should be competent in the field. The head of department whose German lesson was observed by a deputy head who remarked, 'Well I didn't understand one word of that, but it seemed OK to me', was left disappointed and did not advance professionally one jot.

Critical events When considering what to scrutinise carefully, take note of or record in a classroom, the observer has too vast a choice. Myriads of events, some trifling, some more significant, occur even in a single hour. One of the difficulties with some of the checklists and rating schedules, particularly the more quantitative ones, is that they can easily treat all events as equivalent. In the case of the Flanders system, a useful but limited ten category observation schedule developed by Ned Flanders containing items such as 'teacher uses praise', 'teacher gives command' or 'pupil talks in response to teacher', two such different events as the teacher saying 'Open your books' and 'Jump out of the window' would both be recorded in the same way, category 6 'teacher gives command'.

Similar category schedules have yielded valuable information, showing the sheer volume of exchanges in a lesson, revealing that many teachers engage in 1000 or more transactions of one kind or another in a single day, that some teachers never ask questions requiring anything more than the recall of factual information, that some PE teachers use substantial numbers of commands and little else, or that some pupils never take part in any classroom discussion. But for the purpose of teacher appraisal there are other equally valuable options, one of which is the 'critical events' technique. The word 'critical' is a little off putting, perhaps, but the approach itself is quite straightforward and simply requires the observer to look for two or three happenings which seem rather more important than other things which occur. Such critical events do not have to be spectacular, sometimes a smile or a frown may qualify, and they may exert either a positive or negative effect on the lesson, but they must be occurrences related to whatever is the focus of attention.

Amongst the critical events, some commonplace, some more striking, which I have in my own notebooks are: from a study of class management during the first few lessons of the school year a teacher throwing everyone out of his laboratory and making them come in again (he always did this in the first lesson, he explained, just in case there was any ambiguity about who was in charge); a teacher who told off a pupil for chattering to a neighbour and then went over to sit alongside him to help with a difficult problem and re-involved him in his work; and, from a study of teachers' explanations in the primary school, an enthusiastic account in one lesson of how ants milk aphids from a teacher who told me afterwards that this phenomenon had so caught his imagination as a child, he had gone on to specialise in biology at college and had become the science co-ordinator in his school.

One common format for recording critical events is to use the headings: 'What led up to the event?', 'What happened?' and 'What was the outcome?' It is fruitful to discuss such events with the teacher afterwards, and a reasonably neutral way of introducing them is to say something like, 'Near the beginning of the lesson Sally and Marie were sitting at the back of the class and you told them to come and sit at the front nearer your desk. Can you tell me a little more about that?' It is also possible, of course, for the observer to take a less neutral-sounding line.

Lesson discussion Most teachers, having been observed at work, like to have a discussion with the observer, preferably soon after the lesson while it is still fresh in the minds of both. Different observers have their various ways of handling this, some preferring to be directive and to give a list of points they have noted, others inviting teachers to give their reaction to the lesson. There are many questions which may be discussed in such circumstances. These include:

- What was your own reaction to the lesson? Did it appear to go as planned and anticipated?
- In the same circumstances would you do things in the same way? If not what would you change?
- How do you feel the children reacted/behaved in the lesson? Were you satisfied with their contribution and the sort of work they were doing?
- Was this lesson typical of what usually happens with this class or was it different in any significant way?
- Will the topic/work be developed in future lessons? If so, how?

Sometimes immediate discussion of any lessons observed is only one part of what follows, some observers preferring to use a proforma or a notebook with carbon paper so they can give a written copy of their own notes and comments to the teacher. This allows for further discussion at some future date or for any observation to be part of a sustained dialogue about teaching rather than a one-off. Any written notes and oral discussions may then find a natural place as part of an appraisal interview such as is described later in this section.

METHODS OF APPRAISAL 43

Activity 4 Analysing and discussing a lesson

Purpose To explore different ways of analysing and discussing teaching.

Needed A group of people already or likely to be involved in teacher appraisal, preferably at least five or six in any sub-group. A video should be made of a lesson with the following ingredients:
(a) At least 20 minutes where the camera focuses largely on the teacher, preferably including the beginning of the lesson and the end if possible;
(b) A section in the middle where the camera focuses exclusively on individual pupils or small working groups for at least 30 seconds each. Thus a 5 minute section could show ten different individuals or small groups.
(There is a problem with children not used to being filmed who may play up to the cameras, and either a class familiar with video cameras should be found, or children should be filmed on maximum telephoto so that the camera is well away from them. There is an urgent need for good quality professionally, or at least skilfully, made video and films for this purpose).

Activity All members of the group should watch the video but using several different approaches. These might include different individuals:
- Simply making freehand notes of whatever occurs to them.
- Recording notes under headings such as 'class management', 'relationships', 'questioning and explaining', 'pupil response and participation', 'appropriateness of topic and teaching strategies' or whatever is devised.
- Using some kind of rating scale (see p. 44) or checklist.
- Looking for critical events.
- Making notes in such a form that these can be given to the teacher as both a basis for discussion and a record.

Follow-up (a) The group should discuss the different approaches they have used and see what seem to be the positive and negative features of each of them.
(b) A second possibility is for members of the group to role-play the discussion which might follow, either with two members playing the part of teacher and appraiser, or working in pairs to role-play the two parts.

Rating schedules and checklists

A distinction needs to be made here between ratings of personality factors and descriptions of behaviour, which relates to some extent to the discussion on high and low inference measures earlier on page 26. Although there has been considerable interest in teachers' characteristics, particularly in the United States in the 1960s, there is not much evidence that special personality traits such as toughness, eccentricity, radicalness or more generic factors such as extroversion or introversion are very highly correlated with measures of effectiveness. There are so many other factors involved that tend to swamp any individual personality trait or characteristic. In any case, ratings of purely personal characteristics divorced from any consideration of actual classroom behaviour, context or analysis of purpose, can be damaging to individuals, or else make them exceedingly self-conscious. Anyone doubting this should try saying to a teacher one day, 'You seem rather a glum sort of person, try smiling more often.' The result of subsequent smiles through clenched teeth is about as convincing as the average party political broadcast.

It might be interesting at this point to consider the use made of trait and behaviour rating in a different context. Teachers who have been involved in devising pupil profiles will already be familiar with the precepts and associated critiques of these techniques. In business and commerce both kinds of approach have been used extensively. Judith Whyte (1986) in her review of appraisal systems in industry gives two contrasting examples. Figure 1 shows the traditional rating scale of personal qualities with a range of A to E, now declining in usage.

Figure 2 shows a behavioural approach with an itemised scale devised for a manager responsible for the supervision of sales personnel. Scales like this are sometimes known as Behaviourally Anchored Rating Scales (BARS).

Both these examples indicate the sort of instrument that some will not want to touch with several barge poles tied together in the field of teacher appraisal. The sales manager appraisal scale in Figure 2 certainly offers a very powerful form of control, because it is unambiguously clear that anyone seeking a high rating must organise a full day's sales clinic for new recruits. In the much more problematic area of nurturing the nation's youth, I am not sure what single paragon piece of virtue would be placed at the top of such a scale for teachers. It would certainly not be something as simple as organising a one day event. Nor is it clear what set of ascending values should be explicit in a similar exercise for teachers, because the qualities and desirable behaviour teachers may manifest do not always lend themselves to rank ordering in just one straight hierarchical line. The manager scale in Figure 2 switches from

Appraisal In relation to work over the preceding 12 months, place a tick in the appropriate boxes below. *Do not tick against any item which is not strictly relevant to the responsibilities of the job.*

	A	B	C	D	E		Definitions
Performance (output and quality)							
Relations with colleagues and others							A Excellent
Powers of expression							
Initiative							B More than fully meets the standard for the position
Judgement							
Original thought							C Fully meets the standard for the position
Reaction to pressure							
Powers of leadership							D Not fully up to standard required
Ability to delegate, co-ordinate and direct							
Development of subordinates							E Unsatisfactory
Overall rating							*month year*

Give comments where considered necessary.

Figure 1: Traditional appraisal report form. (Reproduced with permission: A.G. Cowling and C.J.B. Mailer (1981). *Managing Human Resources.* London: Edward Arnold.)

46 TEACHER APPRAISAL

Behaviour rating scale of department manager in supervising sales personnel.

	9	
		Conducts a full day's sales clinic with new sales personnel and thereby develops them into top sales people in the department.
Gives his sales personnel confidence and a strong sense of responsibility by delegating many important jobs to them.	8	
	7	Never fails to conduct training meetings with his people weekly at a scheduled hour and to convey to them exactly what he expects.
Exhibits courtesy and respect toward his sales personnel.	6	
	5	Reminds sales personnel to wait on customers instead of conversing with each other.
	4	
Criticises store standards in front of his own people, thereby risking their developing poor attitudes.	3	Orders subordinates to come in even though she/he called in to say she/he was ill
Goes back on a promise to an individual whom he had told could transfer back into a previous department if she/he didn't like the new one.	2	Makes promises to an individual about her/his salary being based on department sales even when he knew such a practice was against company policy.
	1	

(Adapted from J.P. Campbell, M.D. Dunnette, R.D. Arvey and L.V. Hellervik (1973) 'The development and evaluation of behaviourally based rating scales', *Journal of Applied Psychology*, 57, pp. 15–22.)

Figure 2: An example of a behaviourally anchored rating scale. (Reproduced with permission: A.G. Cowling and C.J.B. Mailer (1981). *Managing Human Resources*. London: Edward Arnold.)

uncouth behaviour (breaking promises, criticising people publicly) to thoughtful behaviour (showing courtesy, giving responsibility) at point 4 or 5. Devising such a unidimensional view of, say, a primary teacher, someone working with children who have special educational needs, a deputy head of a secondary school who is responsible for pastoral care, or a lecturer in nuclear physics, would seem to be an unnecessary over-simplification, though a wider set of behaviourally anchored scales might suit some people's needs.

There have been several examples of rating scales being used with teachers. One of the most fully documented which has frequently been used grew out of a massive project in the United States directed by David Ryans (1960). His dimensions, often used since as polar opposites with a five or seven point scale in between, were derived from questionnaires given to thousands of teachers and the observation of many lessons. Some of the most salient characteristics identified by Ryans, set out below, scored for an imaginary teacher on a seven point rating scale, were:

warm, friendly	1 ② 3 4 5 6 7	aloof
systematic, businesslike	1 2 3 4 ⑤ 6 7	unplanned, slipshod
stimulating, imaginative	1 2 ③ 4 5 6 7	dull
favourable attitudes to pupils	1 ② 3 4 5 6 7	unfavourable attitudes to pupils
permissive (child centred)	1 ② 3 4 5 6 7	traditional (learning centred)

These scales suffer inevitably through having been condensed from separate questionnaire items. Thus more specific attitude statements which were used such as 'A teacher should occasionally leave a class to its own management', or 'Learning is more successfully accompanied by group discussion rather than by reading a book on the subject', became compressed into a wide dimension such as permissive/traditional or a false and artificial dichotomy between interest in children or in learning, when it is perfectly possible, and indeed common, to be concerned with both.

This kind of rating scale, if not this actual one, may be helpful if certain conditions are met. It is much easier to use the approach in a research project where larger samples of teachers may be involved and observers trained for long enough to achieve some agreement about the criteria on which any point on the scale will be assigned. It lends itself less successfully to use by someone who has little experience of observing many types of teacher, or in a small intimate school staffroom where it might appear to be too formal and sculptured. Some teachers, of course, might like to have another person's view about how they compare with teachers in similar circumstances or characteristics they or someone they respect judges to be important.

The reasons for cautious use of scaled ratings are well known. They include *halo rating* (the tendency to decide that someone is a 'B' person and give them this grade on nearly every dimension), *recency* (the temptation to be excessively influenced by recent events, so that if someone were to announce to a rater immediately before an appraisal that he was sick of children, the warm/aloof rating might suffer, even if this outburst was not typical of the previous twelve months), and *central clustering* (giving everyone B or C rather than using the full range of the scale). Incidentally I have not mentioned here another kind of scale sometimes used in industrial or commercial contexts, which is *rank ordering,* where an employee is either rank-ordered within the department or unit, or is placed in a category labelled 'Top 10 per cent', '30th to 50th percentile' or some such equivalent. I have assumed that in, say, a small rural primary school, knowing that one is ranked fourth out of four teachers, or in a secondary school knowing that as a history teacher you are ranked above or below a physics or PE teacher, might not perform wonders either for teaching competence or relationships between staff, but more hawkish appraisers might disagree.

Behavioural checklists can be used either with reference to a specific lesson or in more general terms. Three common approaches for lesson observations are:

- *A time line.* Various categories are determined and then, sometimes using graph paper, a time line is drawn showing how long the activity is sustained. To give an oversimplified example, if someone wished to code, during an oral lesson, whether the teacher or a pupil was talking or whether neither was or both were, a time line record might look like this:

teacher talks ___   ___ ___   ___
pupil talks   ___ ___ ___

- *A category system.* A set of categories is drawn up and the list is then tallied each time the event occurs. If a teacher is conducting a public session then, in a simple version, the following sort of record might be produced:

1. Teacher asks question   ✓✓✓✓✓✓✓✓✓✓   11
2. Teacher gives command   ✓✓✓✓   4
3. Teacher uses praise   ✓✓✓✓✓   5
4. Teacher uses criticism   ✓   1

Variations on this include having a very short time period of three or five seconds and simply recording the principal activity within that period, so that if the observer were only using the four categories above, plus zero for when none of these was taking place, then a thirty-second record might look like this, if three second units were used:

| 1 | 1 | 0 | 3 | 0 | 0 | 2 | 0 | 1 | 1 |

- *A sign system*. In this system something is tallied only once if it occurs at all during a fixed time period. If the observer is ticking a set of categories for each two-minute period, for example, then whether a teacher asks ten questions or one the category 'teacher asks question' would only be ticked once. Again in a very much oversimplified form a ten-minute record of a lesson based on five two-minute segments (the thick line after three segments is simply to help observers see which segment they are recording in, because with a large set of categories to tally it can become difficult) might appear thus:

Teacher uses demonstration			✓		
Teacher uses visual aid	✓			✓	✓
Teacher uses analogy			✓		
Teacher explains concept	✓				

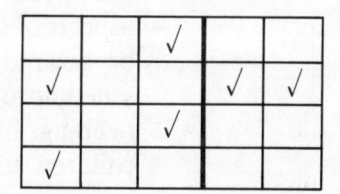

Having a few pages full of ticks, crosses and category totals is not in itself especially useful, in view of the points made above in Section 1 about the absence of hard empirical evidence that any particular piece of teacher or pupil behaviour is invariably and in every context associated with children's learning. An observer may sometimes feel intuitively that a teacher is talking too much and that the class is beginning to feel restless. Neither behavioural checklists nor the research literature offer a foolproof guide to what constitutes 'too much' in a specific context, but skilfully used and as part of many forms of record and feedback, some quantitative or categorised information can help teachers appraise their own lessons. What has been said about the need for training should observers wish to use rating scales certainly applies to behavioural checklists as well. Observers could easily misuse such data and falsely give a teacher the impression that the information had more authority than was really the case.

It could well be that, in the first instance, a school embarking on appraisal may feel that an utterly simple, informal approach is necessary, and that any detailed consideration of systematic approaches is unnecessary. However, once schools move to a level of sophistication where teachers are asking for much more detailed appraisal procedures, with regular analysis and feedback being a central and sustained element rather than a ritualised one-off annual event, a more detailed and systematic way of operating may become essential. Many may also wish to become sophisticated in the art of observation and analysis and learn to use the wide range of qualitative techniques available and described in the books on classroom interaction by writers such as Hammersley (1986a, b).

Peer appraisal and self-appraisal

Many of the procedures described above are appropriate either for self-analysis or for two teachers who wish to work together. They are not exclusively the tools of superiors appraising underlings. Some checklists for self-appraisal might be too formidable for teachers without a proper support system. Over the years local authorities have often set up working parties to produce these, as was mentioned in Section 1, and many offer sensible indicators of aspects of a teacher's work worth further scrutiny. One does need to be aware, however, of the potentially demoralising effect if the schedule of topics and items is too full. One such list has twenty headings on class management alone, with items like 'I never allow children to disrupt my lessons'. All of us would find ourselves somewhat shamefaced by item six, and even St Francis of Assisi and Socrates might be feeling guilty by item ten, so overkill is to be avoided.

What teachers working on their own or in pairs often do need, however, is some degree of structure. During the Teacher Education Project we developed numerous activities for two people to work together or for teachers to analyse their own teaching and these ideas are published in the Macmillan Focus series from 1981 onwards under titles such as *Class Management and Control, Effective Questioning, Teaching Slow Learners in Mixed Ability Classes, Handling Classroom Groups,* as well as guides in the teaching of subjects such as mathematics, science, modern languages and English; the list is given in the Bibliography. A typical exercise for two teachers working together is shown on page 51. In this case the focus is on helping each other improve classroom vigilance and is taken from the booklet on class management.

METHODS OF APPRAISAL 51

FOCUS 2
VIGILANCE

WHEN TO DO THIS: Early on, preferably during the first three weeks of term.

WHO FILLS THIS IN: A fellow student on teaching practice with you, or a fellow teacher.

WHAT TO DO: Select a lesson which will involve something more than just whole class teaching, e.g. small group work, individual work, laboratory experiments. Teach the class normally. Ask a fellow student to fill in the analysis section below. Make sure that the student who does this observation is clear about what is involved.

ANALYSIS

Date _____

Class _____

Subject _____

(*To the observer:* Make brief notes about the lesson in the spaces below. Look through the whole schedule so that you know what must be done during the lesson.)

A. EYES For approximately the *first ten minutes* of the lesson watch the teacher's eyes. Does he/she look at the class when explaining or questioning? When children are working alone or in groups does the teacher look around the room or only at the nearest group?

B. INDIVIDUAL CHILDREN Choose two children who do not appear to be applying themselves to their task. Study these two carefully and make notes about their behaviour. What do they do? What contacts do they have with the teacher? Do they solicit these or does the teacher? Is there any indication from what you see or hear as to *why they are not involved* in their work?

Child A Name _____ (if known, if not brief description)

Child B Name _____ (if known, if not brief description)

> **FOLLOW UP**
>
> 1 Discuss the analysis with your colleague. How vigilant do you seem to have been. Are you surprised at the reports on the two children in B? Did you see most of what the observer describes?
>
> 2 *Eye contact* Try to keep as many children as possible in view when doing whole class teaching, explaining, asking questions etc. Imagine, in other lessons when you are on your own, that an observer is present looking for pupils who have lost interest in the lesson.
>
> 3 *Dividing attention* Try *quite deliberately* to cast an eye occasionally over the rest of the class when you work with an individual or small group. Take immediate action if necessary.
>
> 4 Swap roles with your colleague so that you now do this exercise in his lesson, if possible.

In the minds of those who wish to see a sharp cutting edge, peer or self-appraisal are the soft options, but well done they can be extremely trenchant and effective, eliciting a high degree of commitment from teachers who clearly have a large personal stake. It depends whether teacher appraisal is perceived as a single act perpetrated in ritualised circumstances by a superior on a subordinate. If it is seen much more as a continuous process, then the kind of fine grain critique of one's own or a colleague's professional work followed by some modest piece of action designed to improve skill, as described above, is an essential ingredient. In my view the single event appraisal has limited value. The analogy would be with formal assessment of pupils through written examinations. Children would learn little if they had no schooling but only a cursory examination once a year. Much of the critical appraisal of pupils' work takes place on a day-to-day basis, sometimes with a formal mark, more often with a word of advice, a smile, a raised eyebrow, or a discussion of work in process.

If a central part of appraisal, therefore, is giving teachers regular feedback about their work, not merely calling them to account once every year or two, then this raises once more the place of the perceptions of pupils in each teacher's class, which was mentioned in Section 1. I should be strongly opposed to the use of a grade given by a class as part of an appraisal, but not averse to the use of systematically obtained feedback. To some extent teachers should in any case be obtaining such information, because the questions they ask often reveal whether a class is clear about the topic or is uncomprehending. However, a passing 'Does everybody understand?' will not always produce a response, as some pupils, especially during adolescence, are reluctant to distinguish themselves from their peers.

It is worth considering, therefore, some different forms of pupil response. There are several possibilities.

Class discussion   Depending on the age and disposition of the class there can be some value in a whole class discussion occasionally on how the group feels about its programme of work. Sometimes this will not proceed far beyond the perfunctory, 'It's OK' or 'It's boring, innit', and may not be fruitful. Some pupils role-play, others are reluctant to speak their views in public, but it can be valuable.

Small group   Some teachers prefer to use a smaller group as a thermometer, say half a dozen pupils, boys and girls of varying ability and interest, to stay behind from time to time, answer questions the teacher may ask or simply discuss what the whole class is doing, a sort of informal teacher–pupil committee. This can be a useful forum, because it avoids some of the problems of the whole class bear garden, and allows a sensible discussion of matters such as 'Is what we are doing interesting, valuable?', 'Is it too easy or too hard for some pupils?', 'Am I explaining things clearly?', 'Is there anything which anyone is unhappy about or are there any grumbles or complaints we can talk about?' Provided it does not appear neurotic or masochistic these questions can, of course, be addressed to individuals, and though a teacher too anxious to please or appearing too uncertain or lacking in confidence might undermine a class's faith, in most cases pupils appreciate having a stake in what goes on, and negotiating the curriculum is supposed to be a central precept in both primary education and secondary initiatives such as the Technical and Vocational Initiative (TVEI).

Questionnaire   Since many pupils prefer to write an honest account of their perceptions rather than be asked to utter them publicly, there might be a place for some kind of written feedback. Some teachers like to hand out a small slip of paper from time to time about some specific activity. It is not something to be done on every occasion, but once in a while or for a special reason. It might involve a particular project or topic which has been undertaken, a field trip, a set of lessons introducing and developing a new concept or set of skills, or reaction to the several elements of a 'circus', that is a set of related activities taken in rotation (for example, a class might spend a few weeks on each of 'fabrics', 'plastics', 'microelectronics', 'metalwork' etc. as part of an introductory year in the field of craft, design and technology). Such a response might simply involve a pupil writing under headings, or responding to three or five point scales such as:

The organisation was: VERY GOOD   GOOD   OK   POOR   VERY POOR
The topic for me was: TOO EASY   ABOUT RIGHT   TOO DIFFICULT

Where such scales are used it is important that pupils should also be given a freehand opportunity to say why they gave particular ratings. Another possibility is to write under headings such as 'I particularly enjoyed (or found useful)' or 'I did not enjoy ...'. Since enjoyment is not always a prerequisite for learning, there are other ways in which one can focus on the possible value of what was done, but the request for both positive and negative reactions is worth making, otherwise such written responses can be too ingratiating or too deprecating. It is also worth inviting suggestions about how the activity might be improved if another group were to do the same thing.

Teachers wishing to have direct feedback about themselves as practitioners, rather than the more oblique reaction via responses to activities or projects, might be bold enough to use an itemised questionnaire which focuses on specific aspects of classroom life. One possibility here is to construct a 'My Teacher' questionnaire, simply a set of statements written in a form suitable for the group concerned, containing items which cover matters thought to be important. These can invite yes/no responses, or an answer on a scale of frequency, such as: almost always – usually – sometimes – rarely – almost never. Typical items, with variations according to the age and ability of the children concerned, might be:

My teacher	is usually interested in our work	YES	NO
	helps slower children in a nice way	YES	NO
	tries to be fair to all of us and not have favourites	YES	NO
	explains new work clearly	YES	NO

Many classes can give valuable insights, and teachers willing to put their teaching up for this kind of scrutiny can often learn a great deal. Children usually prefer to fill in such questionnaires anonymously, and some, it must be said, will send up the whole idea if they so decide. Activity 5 invites a closer scrutiny of feedback from other than professional sources. It is essentially an agenda for discussion with an optional activity. It should, incidentally, be discussed as far as possible with an open mind.

METHODS OF APPRAISAL 55

Activity 5 Other perspectives, feedback from non-professionals

Purpose To explore sources of feedback about teaching from pupils and others not working in the education service.

Task Discuss the pros and cons of obtaining feedback about teaching from:
(a) pupils;
(b) parents;
(c) governors;
(d) other members of the community.

Optional activity Construct a feedback sheet or questionnaire of the kind described above for eliciting a written response from pupils. For a feedback sheet choose an activity/module/course suitable for the children with whom the group is concerned. For the questionnaire devise three or four items around each of various key notions such as 'fairness', 'teaching skills', 'pastoral care', 'relationships' or whatever the group judges to be important.

Interviews The word 'interview' has a fairly formal connotation. After all, it is the event which probably helped teachers obtain their present post, and it is usually something one dresses up for. It is often, though not inevitably, a hierarchical event, in that those being interviewed are ushered in, told where to sit, asked questions and eventually some signal from the interviewers tells the interviewee that the episode is over. Take the following short statement: 'Look Fothergill, I've been thinking how we can make best use of you'. Can there be much doubt about who is in control? Is it not likely that two men are involved, and that one is the boss of the other, rather older and more formal perhaps? Of one thing you can be sure: it is not being uttered by a 23-year-old probationer to a 55-year-old Head, at least not by one who is likely to stay for very long.

Interviewing is one of the oldest known human techniques for eliciting or giving information. It is, on the surface, a simple enough affair: A wishes to tell or ask B something, so they meet and a conversation takes place. Yet it is occasionally so badly mismanaged that a scar is left. Most people can recall a bruising, a clumsily delivered message, an uncomfortable experience of one kind or another, possibly a deserved telling off, but sometimes merely an event that was badly managed.

The appraisal interview could easily, if mishandled, achieve the opposite of what is intended, discourage rather than encourage, or alienate rather than win support or goodwill. This raises the question of the purpose of an interview as part of the appraisal procedure. It could be argued that, especially in smaller schools, people have informal conversations every day, so there is little or no need for a more formal event. Yet a quiet period away from others, when teachers can have a sustained conversation, both retrospective about their career so far, and prospective about how they might develop, provided it is held with someone who not only knows about their work but cares about it, seems to be a minimum professional right. Even if there are countless informal exchanges, an occasional more deliberate and slightly more formal event is worthwhile.

There are numerous ways of conducting an interview. The environment can be important, and subtle signals, where and how each person sits, who leads whom, smiles, nods, frowns, vacant expressions, are not usually missed by participants. The interview can either be *tightly structured* with numerous short questions requiring yes/no or brief factual answers (How many lessons of X do you teach? Have you been on an in-service course this year?), or it can be *unstructured,* simply an open agenda conversation with no predetermined format, or it may be *semi-structured* with a set of headings such as 'Satisfaction or otherwise with present teaching programme', 'Criticisms or suggestions about school organisation'. My own preference would be for the semi-structured format as being one that allowed freedom for a genuine exchange of views or advice, but had enough shape to avoid a formless and aimless drift.

Any group considering the place of one or more interviews as part of an appraisal procedure might, therefore, need to address some of the following questions:

- *When should interviews take place?* How often, once a year for something a little more organised than informal conversations? Should it be early or late in the year? Should it precede or follow any formal written appraisal?
- *Who should conduct the interview?* Should it always be done by a superior? Should it be the Head, the deputy head, an adviser or other outsider? Should heads of departments in secondary schools and teachers with special responsibility in primary schools be responsible for conducting some interviews? Should anyone else be present, a colleague, a union adviser, a governor?
- *What should be the principal purpose of the interview?* Should it be mainly retrospective, reviewing the previous year or two, or someone's career in the school to date? Should it also look ahead;

if so, how far, one year only, a longer view? Should it be one-way or two-way (opportunity for the teacher to comment on the running of the school, department or both, and its principal objectives)?
- *What should be the structure and content of the interview?* Should it be completely open? Should there be predetermined headings; if so, what might these cover?
Present teaching programme and satisfaction or dissatisfaction?
Classroom skills, including teacher's knowledge of relevant subject(s), bringing in any lesson observation or feedback from other sources?
General and administrative responsibilities within school and extra-curricular activities?
Relationships with staff, pupils, parents, others?
In-service and professional development needs?
Career advice?
Teacher's own advice on improving and view of the running of the school/department?
Other?
- *Should it be recorded in written form?* Should there be some written account of the interview, either with the interviewer's actual notes taken during the interview or a report summarising these? Should the account be seen and verified by the teacher concerned? What should happen to these written copies?

There is one further point which must be made here, and it is a very important one. Whatever the ostensible purpose of any interview it is common for it to become a vehicle for all kinds of other purpose: a chance to express a grievance, make a suggestion, engage in (often mutually) therapeutic talk, sometimes to the point of windbaggery, even slip the knife into an unpopular colleague. It has already been pointed out in Section 1 that in the 1990s most teachers will be over 40 and that teacher appraisal needs to be undertaken in a way that reflects a mature profession. However, people in their forties may be facing difficulties which did not affect them in their thirties. These include coping with teenage children of their own, with elderly and perhaps ailing parents or other close relatives, with being a single parent, with a broken or disintegrating marriage or relationship, with stresses of other kinds, with disillusionment from lack of promotion and uncertainty about the future, or with ill health, physical or mental, of their own. Though some people are spared these problems in early or later middle age, many others are not. Hopes and aspirations or problems and disaffection at work cannot be divorced entirely from similar problems in a person's private life. In some cases the person with home and family problems may also be the primary teacher whose maths work is a disaster, the head of modern languages whose own spoken French is poor, or the science co-ordinator whose newly arrived probationer knows more than he does. Those conducting interviews of the kind described above, therefore, will have to be exceptionally skilful both at handling the actual situation, and also knowing when to probe, when to leave alone, when to encourage and when to act firmly. It will be one of the most important and demanding assignments to be faced by many working at a more senior level in schools and in the education service generally.

Using educational technology

This is but a short note, as the subject is too vast to cover in any detail here, but there has been mention from time to time of using a video or some other hinted application of modern information technology.

Tape recorders These can be useful for making sound recordings of lessons. Usually there is so much background noise, especially in uncarpeted areas, that tapes of lessons are useless, especially if there is no logical place to site a microphone, and few schools can afford the several hundred pounds necessary to buy a radio-microphone carried by the teacher. On the other hand, a tape recorder on a teacher's desk can sometimes give a reminder of a lesson if listened to shortly afterwards, and can be useful in self-appraisal, where teachers are listening to their own lesson.

Another question to ask is whether appraisal interviews should be taped. Some people are strongly averse to speaking in the presence of a tape recorder, there always being an uncomfortable feeling that the tapes might be played back to someone else who would not understand the context or might misuse them in some way. It is possible that some teachers might actually want a taped record of their interview for future reference. It is also possible, of course, to role-play and record an appraisal interview and then play it back for a group discussion about the nature and role of such an interview.

Video cameras The most recent video cameras for home and amateur use can be extremely valuable in schools, especially as the compact ones contain the cassette and the microphone within them, and are self-focusing, needing neither a separate recorder nor an operator if set on wide angle in a classroom. The results are not perfect, but a reasonable picture of classroom life can be captured. Although some children play up to a camera in the early stages, it becomes largely ignored if present on a regular basis.

Possible uses include:

- Teachers using the camera for self-appraisal, recording from a position which is not too obtrusive but encompasses much of the teaching area, and then analysing their own teaching at some subsequent viewing.
- A similar use, but for discussion with others about improving what the teacher does.
- Making videos for in-service purposes or for appraisal planning sessions; these can be either actual or role-played events.

The presence of a visual as well as a sound record of a lesson makes this a more useful tool than the tape recorder, but the sound may still be unclear, especially if a camera set at the back of a class does not pick up clearly the sound of events at the front, particularly those involving the teacher. More sophisticated arrangements involving two cameras, a split screen, or using more than one microphone are possible, but at present beyond the means of most schools, and could in any case become too intrusive.

Microcomputer/word processors Large schools may be contemplating the use of microcomputers or word processors, and with substantial numbers of teachers this may help reduce the bureaucracy. There are some reservations, however, which need to be borne in mind. First of all it would be time-saving if reports written about a teacher, and subsequently amended following an interview, or if the teacher had pointed out erroneous statements, were typed on a word processor. Hard-pressed school secretaries would not have to retype endless sheets of corrections. It must be remembered that word processors are also subject to Data Protection legislation, and, depending on what use is to be made, for example if a report is to be kept on disc, the teacher concerned will probably have to see the record. A second point concerns the use of standardised templates or outlines. Most teachers will see appraisal as a sensitive and personalised matter. Any sense that one is part of an unfeeling automated process will only create ill will. The sort of perfunctory machine-printed 'This teacher (insert name) is generally (insert adjective), but can occasionally be (insert another adjective)' may simply alienate teachers or alternatively lead them to mock the silly bureaucratic nature of the exercise. Word processors do not have to be used as crassly as this. I end this section as I began it by repeating that none of the procedures described above is idiot-proof and that intelligent and thoughtful application is essential.

Part 3 The implementation of teacher appraisal

It has been made clear in the preceding Sections that a local authority and its individual schools need to have clear policies about the purpose and nature of teacher appraisal schemes, however informal these may be in practice, especially where they show individual variations from school to school. In their 1985 pamphlet *Quality in Schools*, HMI reported that appraisal schemes appeared to work best where the school as a whole was accustomed to looking critically at its practices. This remark emphasises that the appraisal of individual teachers cannot and should not be isolated from scrutiny of the school as an organic whole. There is an aide-memoire used by HMI when looking at teacher appraisal schemes and also one for considering school self-evaluation, and these are reproduced in Appendix A. Both pose pertinent questions which can be usefully asked by those determining appraisal procedures.

The increasing scope of teachers' skills

The role of the teacher in recent times has expanded considerably. It is not uncommon to see a teacher working in a difficult inner-city school stand up at a national conference and say, 'I trained as a teacher, not as a social worker'. Teachers can find themselves filling several roles in any one day and they probably received training for few of them. These include: subject expert, guidance counsellor, jailer (in a high truancy area), first aider when accidents occur, manager of resources, team member, assessor (of pupils' progress and now, perhaps, of their own colleagues), surrogate parent, social worker or community liaison worker. No individual could excel in all these fields, and it is for those involved in teacher appraisal to help determine which aspects of any teacher's job are most important, which peripheral and which outside the remit of the post concerned.

Many of the wider aspects of a teacher's job were covered in Section 2, but it would be easy to overlook some of the following.

Pastoral care Many teachers do valuable work in this field which may not be apparent either during classroom observation or in an interview, especially when teachers are modest and unpretentious about what they do. Often valuable contacts with children occur outside lesson time, perhaps in the corridor, school yard, a quiet corner after school, and some may be confidential or private, not the substance of staffroom conversation. An honest self-report may give a better picture of what can often be elusive, and, occasionally, illusory. In general there should be some clear indication of what is expected of, say, a class teacher or a form group tutor, which can be checked out with individuals.

Assessment of pupils' work Although formal tests or examinations may bring a teacher's assessment under more public scrutiny, much of it is unspectacular and routine. A senior person in the school is entitled to ask about assessment and record keeping, and it is perhaps a topic which can be explored in an interview more effectively than in other contexts.

Relations with others Most teachers have to establish and maintain relationships with fellow adults as well as children on a daily basis. Amongst these 'significant others' are senior staff in a school, colleagues in the same department in a secondary school, or cooperating fellow teachers in a primary school, visitors to the school, either professional people such as advisers, tutors visiting students, speech therapists, or lay people like parents and governors, and employees such as ancillary classroom assistants and caretakers. Indeed, so monumentally important were relationships with the last of these that many 'in-tray' exercises for training Heads and senior staff have consisted of letters about rows between the caretaker and the art teacher. Again this is a matter which can be taken up during informal conversations or more formal interview. The question of relationships may also be of especial concern in certain kinds of school. Teachers in schools serving children from several different ethnic groups may do excellent community relations work which should be given due recognition. Similarly those teaching in community schools and colleges may have an effect well beyond the confines of their own classroom.

Appraising senior staff It is one thing for a person in a senior position to appraise someone more junior, but quite another matter when it comes to the appraisal of senior staff. In a primary school a Head or deputy will usually have been a class teacher and ought therefore to be knowledgeable about what is involved, and in secondary schools a head of department ought to be expert in the teaching of the subject concerned, but when it comes to these key senior people being themselves appraised there are certain difficulties. A primary adviser may not have been a primary Head; a secondary Head who is an historian might know plenty about running a department, but relatively little about the teaching of physics or modern languages. Finding someone with expert knowledge in the field, equivalent professional experience and in the right position to undertake what could be one of the most sensitive acts of appraisal in the whole system will in some cases be very difficult.

So far as subject specialist coordinators in primary schools and heads of department in secondary schools are concerned there is clearly a role for local authority advisers and inspectors. The time considerations will be ferocious here, and these will be discussed further below. One possibility would be for more 'advisory teachers' to be appointed, possibly on a three-year assignment, and for them to undertake such work on a regular basis. When it comes to deputy heads then head teachers themselves should have a good idea of what the job entails, though it would be unfair if evaluation rested entirely with them, so an external input may be necessary. Some occasional release of heads of departments, primary subject coordinators and deputy heads to visit equivalent post holders in other schools can also be considered.

With appraisal of Heads themselves particular care is needed, as by overwhelming agreement the quality of leadership offered by the Head of a school is of crucial importance. The Suffolk Education Department (1985 and 1987) in its useful studies of teacher appraisal proposes that, since appraisers should know by their own experience rather than vicariously what is involved in any post, a new category of 'promoted head' is required, rather than a retired head or former HMI. This could have some attractions, provided it was seen by all concerned to be an important post. Heads themselves would have to regard the job as an honourable one, so that outstanding Heads came forward to do it and that their fellow Heads respected the people chosen. Nothing would be worse than for the post to be perceived as a reward for old lags, a device for cooling out Heads who were running too hot in their own school, or a consolation prize for someone whose school has been closed or reorganised.

Since even the most seasoned practitioners can easily lose touch with the day-to-day problems of running a school after time away from it, perhaps the appointment of such superordinate Heads should be for a limited period, perhaps a minimum of two and a maximum of four years.

The question of criteria on which judgement should be based is also relevant here. Heads of schools carry wide responsibilities. In addition to the duties of many classroom teachers they have further, and in some cases the final, responsibility for:

- The assigning and maintenance of resources, both human and material.
- Children's safety and welfare.
- Dealing with outside agencies such as the local authority, examination boards, HMI, parents' organisations, the press, pressure groups.
- Liaising with parallel professional operations like social services, probationary service, medical and health services, educational psychologists.
- School administration, accounts and finances.
- Staff and ancillary appointments.
- Policy formation and implementation.
- Pastoral care, assessment, curriculum construction, implementation and evaluation.

For many Heads in particular, and to some extent deputies and senior teachers, this list is an understatement. The appraisal of competence in such a wide and diverse set of responsibilities cannot be achieved by a single method, instrument or on a single occasion. Nor do job descriptions, where they exist, always help. Common sense sometimes decrees that certain things must be done whether they are written down or not. During periods of industrial action senior teachers, deputies and Heads have to make many difficult decisions, few of which can have been put to them when they applied for their post or were written down on paper.

Dr Michael Youngman (1984) of Nottingham University analysed what senior secondary teachers actually do when they manage staff or manage the teaching of others, based on interviews and questionnaire responses from several hundred teachers. He found many aspects which do not always figure in written job descriptions. Under 'managing staff' he found senior teachers chairing meetings, evaluating teaching, reprimanding staff if necessary, delegating tasks to others, serving on school committees and writing references. Under the heading 'managing the teaching of others' he listed thirteen different activities:

    select examination board
    check testing and marking of other teachers
    liaise with departments in further or higher education
    compile timetable for student teacher
    participate in selection of new staff
    write references for staff
    compile documentation on student or probationer in difficulty

compile room timetable
allocate staff to classes
arrange for staff to attend courses
maintain record of marks of other staff
explain option-choice arrangement to staff
decide allocation of rooms to staff

Not all of these are equivalent, nor are they invariably carried out by all senior staff, but clearly some senior people do undertake several such activities. If they do the important ones skilfully this should be to their credit; if they fail to carry out crucial duties then the appraisal interview might be used partially to call them to account and to help them discharge their duties more effectively.

Much of what has been said, therefore, in the previous pages applies to the appraisal of senior people as well: that it is a sensitive matter involving mature professionals, that the form of appraisal needs to be clear, that it should be undertaken by people who understand the job, or in the case of subject specialists, know the field, that a semi-structured interview is useful even if there are many informal conversations, that it should be part of a concern for improving what the whole school does, and that it should be open and reciprocal, which rules in the possibility of incorporating feedback from more junior people. I would strongly urge senior people conducting appraisal interviews to invite those with whom they speak to offer suggestions about how they can improve their management skills, as well as logging and dealing with complaints as the need arises. Not all feedback to appraisers about themselves should come from above. Consequently the appraisal of senior people may take more time and this is further discussed below.

Differences between primary and secondary schools

Peter Delaney (1986) has written an engaging account of how the Salford primary school, of which he is the Head, introduced and carried out an appraisal policy. He tells how the staff worked together to establish an acceptable system. Much of what he describes could as easily have been done in a secondary school context. At the same time the intimacy of what is usually a smaller unit results from a difference in scale which in turn often requires less formality than a large secondary school with perhaps 80 or more staff.

Other distinctions are not always as sharp as they once were. For example, there has traditionally been more emphasis on subject specialism in secondary schools, but in more recent times special postholders have been appointed in primary schools to coordinate their colleagues' efforts, and in some cases teach their classes, particularly in subjects such as mathematics, science, music and

French. Mixed ability groups, at one time common in primary schools, but less in evidence thereafter, have now become widespread in the early years of secondary schooling. Indeed it is remarkable how many similarities there are between what has for long been regarded as good primary practice and some of the key precepts of the Technical and Vocational Initiative (TVEI) for 14 to 18 year olds, such as experience-led learning, the negotiated curriculum, collaborative teamwork, integrated project and topic work rather than solely single subject learning, and pupil profiling.

Nonetheless there will still be some significant differences between the two sectors, and this will be especially noticeable at the extremes, the very large secondary school compared with the very small village primary school. The implementation of appraisal in primary and secondary schools may proceed as follows.

Primary schools Whole staff discussion of the purposes of appraisal – possible involvement with other similar schools (especially important in scattered rural areas where several schools may work as a federation, and where appraisers need to understand the particular problems facing a two, three or four teacher school covering a curriculum and teaching a wide age span, often with few resources) – discussion of style of appraisal in the light of LEA guidelines or proposed federation practice – exploration of the use of pupil feedback (bearing in mind that younger children may be less fluent in the written mode), and classroom observation, trying out different approaches and if possible visiting other schools – decisions about written form of any appraisal, use of appraisal interview, involvement of advisory service or other outsiders – discussion about in-service and professional development needs likely to arise (there is further discussion below of this topic) – explaining appraisal scheme to be used to governors and parents as appropriate – implementation of agreed procedures on a trial basis with evaluation and subsequent modification in the light of experience.

Secondary schools Whole staff discussion, with smaller working groups if necessary, on the purposes of appraisal – discussion within departments or faculties of subject specialist matters – exploration in the light of LEA guidelines of whole school practice plus any subject variations, and consideration of pupil feedback, classroom observation, trying out different approaches – visits to other schools if possible on a peer basis; for example, deputy head goes to see fellow deputy head to discuss matters of common interest, head of department visits counterpart in similar school to compare preliminary thoughts and likely practice – decisions about written form of any appraisal, use of appraisal interview, involvement of advisory service or other outsiders – discussion about in-service and professional development needs likely to arise – explaining appraisal scheme to be used to governors and parents (and possibly to pupils) as appropriate – implementation of agreed procedure on a trial basis with evaluation and subsequent modification in the light of experience.

In addition there will be variations between schools in the light of their style of management and school objectives. Those schools which give prominence to written objectives, or where there is belief in management by objectives, will no doubt devise a scheme which includes scrutiny of the extent to which individual teachers and the school as a whole are achieving these. Where objectives are less explicit they will either become more so, or a different style of appraisal will evolve. If secondary schools in particular are more hierarchical in organisational structure than primary schools, they are more likely to use what some people call the 'father–grandfather' approach.

Aftercare: in-service and professional development

A system of appraisal which was entirely backward-looking and punitive would be useless so far as the encouragement of change is concerned. If appraisal is to have a proper cutting edge, if it is to be a genuine evaluation of what takes place with a view to improving the quality of teaching and therefore of pupil learning and opportunities, then there must be a properly conceived structure for aftercare. It would be grossly unfair for someone to write an appraisal of a primary teacher, say, which proclaimed 'Language and number work excellent, topics and projects well conceived, relationships with class good, contribution to life of school excellent, science work cursory and barely existent', and then leave the teacher concerned unsupported. The teacher would almost certainly reply that he never did any science in his own training and that what he would dearly like to do is take the one term full-time professional certificate course in 'Science and technology in the primary school' offered at his local College of Higher Education.

It must be further recognised that improving teachers' skills requires them to change their behaviour in some way. Yet the evidence from classroom observation research shows that teaching can be an exceptionally busy job with little time to reflect during the many rapid-fire transactions which can take place in even a single day. Furthermore, many teachers develop fixed and regular patterns of interaction with their classes. Given the mature teaching profession we shall have during the last years of the 1980s and well into the 1990s this means that many teachers who are appraised, and expected to make major or minor changes in their teaching styles as a result, will have had literally millions of repeats and rehearsals of whatever have become their favoured teaching strategies. When circumstances change, when there is a new curriculum, a change in the age or ability level of the pupils being taught, a new examination like the General Certificate of Secondary Education, or a change in the objectives of the school or department, then either no in-service at all or a brief day or two on assessment techniques has about as much impact on helping teachers change their behaviour as a grain of sand hitting the ocean.

The professional development of teachers, therefore, needs to be central, not peripheral in the appraisal process. It should certainly figure prominently in informal discussions as well as any more formal appraisal interview or written report. What is more there should be a follow-up check at some future date, either after a year or at a subsequent appraisal, to see whether action has been taken. The obligation is both on individual teachers to attend courses or otherwise work at their teaching, and on the school and local authority to provide appropriate support. Large schools which have a professional tutor, or person given responsibility for professional development, will find there is a real job to do. Indeed, I have constantly stressed in this guide that the business of improving the quality of what is done is a whole school matter. A former research assistant of mine is now a primary school teacher. Her experience analysing teachers' explaining skill is now invaluable to a school which is anxious that all teachers should learn to analyse and improve their own teaching as part of the continuous, rather than ritualised, appraisal process.

This need for professional support certainly extends to Heads and other senior teachers; it is not solely for novices or those facing change in the classroom. At Nottingham University part-time modular courses for deputy heads which allowed them to analyse a department in their own school, study a particular class or group of pupils, visit the school of a fellow deputy to see how that school handled pastoral care or innovation in the curriculum, were very much appreciated as ways of developing professional expertise in mature people who were already very skilled but still eager to improve. Indeed, the introduction of formal appraisal itself will put extra demands on senior people, and their ability to observe lessons, chair meetings looking at appraisal issues, write reports, conduct sensitive and positive interviews and evaluate progress will be most important in the success or failure of teacher appraisal, so they too must be supported as they seek to develop, nurture or extend the relevant expertise. Since April 1987, when the in-service funding arrangements changed, some local authorities have given schools their own in-service budget, but it may be well short of what is needed when a school has introduced a fully-fledged appraisal scheme.

Cost implications: time and money

It is customary for government ministers to assume that any new developments can be implemented within existing resources or with little extra cash by simply eradicating certain inefficiencies in the system, and for local authorities and teacher unions to insist that only the injection of a million trillion pounds will ensure the success of the novelty. Both have a point, but something as substantial as developing a properly conceived teacher appraisal scheme where in many cases none exists, does have considerable implications, both in terms of time and money. The Suffolk Education Department (1985) pamphlet on appraisal lists the following guidelines for LEAs and schools. The cost implication of many of its features are sizeable.

GUIDELINES

All teacher appraisal schemes should:

- Be given high organisational priority by the L.E.A. as a contribution to the positive and efficient management and deployment of its teaching force.

- Provide a handbook giving details of the whole process.

- Ensure that seven main phases are adequately implemented:
  Preparation; Classroom Observation; Appraisal Interview; Results; Monitoring; Moderation; Evaluation.

- Ensure that professional associations are fully consulted and involved.

- Ensure that each school encourages the maximum participation of teachers in the planning and operation of the process.

- Establish criteria by which a teacher's work is appraised and ensure that these criteria are disseminated and fully understood.

- Ensure that those being appraised have the opportunity to participate in each phase of the process, and that attention is paid to the particular needs of each teacher.

- Provide documents for the teacher and the appraiser, with notes for guidance.

- Provide sufficient time for data to be gathered.

- Ensure that all appraisals relate to a clear and up-dated job description which covers the range of responsibilities devolved upon the teacher concerned.

- Provide realistic targets which have been agreed between the teacher and the appraiser.

- Provide support and training so that targets can be attained.

- Ensure consistency within and between schools by setting up machinery for moderating the scheme, drawing personnel specifically for the task from its officers, advisers, headteachers and senior teaching staff.
- Ensure that such moderating staff receive training in supervision and observation skills.
- Use current grievance procedures for appeals concerning the appraisal process.

The first requirement of many of the points made in this guide is for time: to discuss plans, to observe lessons, to visit other schools, to consult pupils, to write reports, to tell governors and parents, to evaluate progress and modify procedures, to hold interviews, to attend in-service courses. Although time can be taken away from other affairs, there is not much of it spare in most schools at present. Without extra money for teaching to cover the time of those engaged in legitimate appraisal activities it is difficult to see how any scheme can be implemented properly.

Let us take the case of a local authority with 7,000 teachers at all levels from primary school to college, and suppose that each teacher was to be appraised one particular year. Given what has been said above we shall require each teacher to be observed. Teachers understandably argue that there is no point in someone only coming to see them one Friday afternoon when few pupils are interested, after a wet playtime when young children are restless, or when they take 2c who, as everyone knows, are the worst class in the school this year. Perhaps we need to see each teacher more than once, possibly three times to be fair, once each term. The observer must, of course, see a decent amount of teaching, certainly not just a few minutes, an hour possibly as a minimum, and we must not forget the time needed to discuss what the observer has seen, so perhaps a half day is necessary, particularly if the observer has to travel.

So far the bill is 7000 times a half day on three occasions, that is 10,500 working days of somebody's time. It will probably involve a senior person, so the true cost of a single such day with overheads, salary etc. will be near enough £100 at 1987 prices. This excludes the cost of staff meetings, appraisal interviews, writing and reading reports or indeed the substantial costs of any in-service which ensues. The baseline is already over £1,000,000 with an initial cost per classroom teacher of perhaps £100 to £150, more for a senior teacher, and arguably nearer £1000 for Heads if someone is to spend three or four days with them at various stages in the year. No doubt the exercise can be done more cheaply, but whether what resulted would embody the principles of real rather than perfunctory appraisal, with genuine improvements in what children receive in school, is highly unlikely.

Competent and incompetent teachers

I have saved until last one of the most contentious matters, that of dealing with teachers who are confirmed by formal appraisal (for it is probably well known already) as being incompetent or, more happily, those seen to be competent, and this will be the majority according to HMI surveys, or very competent.

Incompetent teachers Teachers who, for whatever reason, are not effective, or are downright incompetent, are an embarrassment to all concerned. Their colleagues suffer because parents complain that there are 'some teachers' in the school who are very poor; their classes, especially in primary schools where there may be no escape, can be thoroughly miserable and put children off a subject for life, or even alienate them from learning at all, and parents will often complain loudly to the Head demanding to know why nothing is done. The bad teachers themselves cannot always be too happy either, unless their defences are so well oiled that they have rationalised the problem out of sight, and either believe it does not exist or that it is the fault of others.

Yet there are few proper studies of such teachers. Perhaps it is the difficulty of knocking on someone's classroom door and announcing, 'I'm conducting research into incompetent teachers and the head has given me your name, so I'd like to come in and see how you do it'. There is, however, one very useful account of some American work by Bridges (1986), and what he reports from 141 school districts in California is of considerable interest. Incompetence, he finds, is of many kinds and occurs for several reasons. Few teachers who pose problems in a school only show one unidimensional inadequacy. Most fall short on several criteria: failing to keep order, impart subject matter effectively, accept advice, treat pupils properly or achieve a reasonable standard of work from them.

One of the major problems documented by Bridges is the sheer cost in time and energy of dealing with incompetence. One school district had calculated the cost in time, energy, counselling services and litigation costs at $166,000 per dismissal. Rather than embark on this crippling journey, many schools resorted to accommodation and even tolerance or protection of poor performers. Heads inflated the annual appraisal rating in areas where two successive 'unsatisfactory' grades meant automatic initiation of dismissal proceedings, so that only one teacher in 300 was given such a grade. Other evasive techniques included transfer to a different class or school, one Head even effecting this on a daily basis, preferring presumably to stay up half the night revamping the timetable rather than face irate parents, or assignments to more non-teaching duties such as library work or administrative chores.

As a consequence actual dismissals were rare, and tended to be in

95 per cent of cases either temporary or probationer teachers. Heads preferred instead to lean on miscreants to obtain what Bridges calls an 'induced exit'. Tactics ranged from gentle persuasion to threats and intimidation, and included bombarding the teachers with every complaint received or sending them on a course with an insistence that they demonstrate a marked improvement on their return. One particular difficulty faced by heads was the teacher with a poor record who could put on a better display when outside evaluators were present.

Local authorities usually have clear guidelines about dealing with incompetence, but they almost always omit certain important details, especially about the reasons for poor teaching. Teachers temporarily up against it in their home or family life, suffering poor health or stress, are not in the same category as seasoned evaders of work who have not the slightest intention of doing a hand's turn of honest endeavour if one of their colleagues will do it instead. The path through appraisal and towards dismissal is rightly long and difficult, because people should not be fired arbitrarily, for a trivial misdemeanour or because some powerful individual dislikes them. For a Head it is especially difficult and a strong local authority presence is essential. For a teacher it usually requires informal warnings, informal discussions about what is going wrong and how it can be rectified, a not too late alerting of someone in the local authority, an adviser or Area Education Officer, that all is not well, the writing of a formal statement to the person spelling out in detail the nature of complaints or criticisms with a request for a written assurance that steps will be taken, a formal written warning, a diary of events kept by the Head or other appropriate person, a final written warning plus the provision of any necessary courses, demonstration by other teachers or professional help, and finally dismissal proceedings. Along the way transfers to other schools may have been effected or considered, and the school governors should have been informed. So far as any formal appraisal is concerned, however, it would have to be clear that the teacher's work was unsatisfactory. Any case coming before an Industrial Tribunal where dismissal was proposed, but the formal appraisal was ambiguous, would no doubt be thrown out and the teacher concerned awarded compensation.

Competent teachers Large-scale primary and secondary surveys by HMI have confirmed that most teachers and most children in most schools work hard; indeed, that was the wording of the DES press release when the secondary school survey was published in 1979, but some newspapers seemed reluctant to quote it. For most teachers, therefore, appraisal should be an opportunity for some congratulation and endorsement, but also an opportunity to build on strengths and rectify weakness or improve aspects where the teacher lacks knowledge or confidence. It should not be over cosy, however, otherwise nothing will change, and schools cannot afford to stand still.

Merit pay This raises the question of paying especially competent teachers more money, a decision which will usually be out of the hands of individual schools and teachers because the existence, removal or extension of such inducements is usually determined at national rather than local level. If there are to be extra payments to those deemed especially good, then the question arises whether these should be awarded as part of the appraisal system or dealt with separately. Whether one likes merit payments or not, if they exist they must be seen to be fairly if not perfectly assigned. It would be perverse, therefore, if the results of appraisal were to be totally ignored when decisions were made. There is, however, one very important message from industry and commerce which needs to be remembered. Judith Whyte (1986) in her review of appraisal in several contexts shows that the evidence elsewhere is that it is not advisable to link directly an appraisal interview with a payment decision. Evidence from studies of the United States General Electric Company and other concerns has shown quite persuasively that *pay reviews* should be separated from *performance reviews* and *potential reviews* (estimating what the person can best do in the future). Mixing pay and appraisal in the same interview is confusing for all concerned, as the roles of counsellor, patron and paymaster become blurred and can produce negative results.

'Merit pay.'

Activity 6 A structure for appraisal

This final activity is based on the two forms for appraisal given on the following pages. The first one below is simply a possible report form such as a school might devise after due deliberation, and which might be filled in at the end of a year during which the teacher had been observed teaching on three occasions by the person completing the report. The task of the group is to discuss it and then:
(a) decide which features or what aspect of the structure would suit the school's own needs;

(b) amend it in any way which would make it more suitable for the school;
(c) if necessary reject if completely and devise a better one.

For those especially interested in working with student or probationer teachers, Appendix B contains the report form which schools are asked to complete on student teachers and the accompanying description of criteria used at the University of Exeter School of Education. The same exercise can be done on this one too. Neither form, incidentally, is offered as a paragon, merely as something to initiate and focus discussion.

APPRAISAL FORM   CONFIDENTIAL

Name of School _____

Name of Teacher _____

A TEACHING SKILLS AND KNOWLEDGE

1. Preparation and planning

2. Class management

3. Communication skills (questioning, explaining etc.)

4. Pupils' work

    (a) appropriateness to age and ability

    (b) quality and degree of progress

5. Assessment of pupils' work and record keeping

6. Knowledge of relevant subject matter

B RELATIONSHIPS

1. with pupils

2. with staff

3. with others

C OTHER PROFESSIONAL CONTRIBUTIONS

1. Extracurricular activities

2. Pastoral responsibilities

3. Other

D APPRAISER'S REPORT

1. What are the teacher's strengths and how might these best be used and developed?

2. Are there aspects of the teacher's work which might need strengthening?

3. What suggestions would you make for in-service and professional development?

4. General comment

5. Tick one of the following

   The teacher's work is satisfactory ☐

   The teacher's work is unsatisfactory ☐

E TEACHER'S REPORT

1. Self-appraisal – comment on your own teaching (including pupils' views if you have elicited these)

2. Comment, if you wish, on the Appraiser's report in Sections A, B and C

3. What support do you feel you might need in the next year

4. Are you satisfied or dissatisfied with your present teaching programme? (Give reasons)

5. Are you satisfied with the way the school is managed and run? (Give reasons)

6. Do you have any suggestions for improving:

   (a) The quality of your own teaching and pupils' learning?

   (b) The quality of what is done in the school and the running of it?

F DECLARATIONS (to be signed by the teacher)

I have read this report and am aware of its contents.

Signed _____ (TEACHER)

I have discussed this report with the teacher.

Signed _____ (APPRAISER)

Date _____

Conclusion

In this guide I have tried to give just a few examples of the kinds of approach which might be used in a teacher appraisal scheme. What has been described is certainly not exhaustive, as there are countless other possibilities, the only limits being the usual ones of time, cost, feasibility, energy and imagination.

Whatever form of appraisal is devised for local authorities or schools should not remain static and unchanged. Actual implementation soon reveals the strengths and limitations of any particular approach, and it is a pity if procedures known to be inadequate or lacking credibility are allowed to persist unaltered. Any school introducing appraisal for the first time, therefore, should regard its initial format as a pilot, subject to modification in the light of experience and feedback from those involved.

My own personal preferences, for what they are worth, have probably been apparent on every page, but let me conclude by summarising what I believe to be important elements of any appraisal scheme. It should:

- Be fully discussed by individual teachers and heads, not just their representatives, before implementation
- Be open, not closed, with teachers able to see and countersign what is written about them
- Involve direct classroom observation, not be based entirely on hearsay
- Include peer review and not be solely derived from superior-subordinate appraisal
- Involve specialists, where subject knowledge or expertise with particular age groups or types of children are important
- Include an external element where appropriate, especially at senior or specialist level, involving advisers, teachers and heads from other schools, but not specially hired evaluators with no other function
- Allow enough time for both appraiser and appraisee to do a proper job
- Include at least one interview
- Offer a sensibly conceived system of aftercare and in-service
- Recognise the pupils' point of view
- Be part of a coherent process of whole school self-evaluation
- Keep governors and parents informed, though not invite them to rate teachers
- Be implemented in a sensitive, not hamfisted, manner
- Be modified in the light of experience
- Result in improved learning opportunities for both children and teachers
- Emphasise improving the quality of teaching rather than bureaucracy or power

APPENDIX A

Aide-memoire used by HMI in relation to school self-evaluation

1. *The purpose of evaluation*

    To improve the functioning of the school?
    In response to specific problems/issues?
    To provide information for accountability?
    Whose initiative?
    How are general and specific objectives established and communicated?
    Is there agreement about the purpose?

2. *The information and judgements required*

    On all aspects of school/college life or is the focus on particular aspects?
    How is the information assembled?
    What emphasis on:
    a. inputs (O + M), staff, resources, planning)?
    b. processes (effectiveness, delivery)?
    c. outputs (pupils' learning)?
    Are criteria explicit where judgements are required?
    Do teachers evaluate their own performance?

3. *The methods used*

    Is it to be a single exercise, a recurrent activity or a continuous rolling programme?
    How detailed is the prescribed or recommended structure?
    Aide-memoires, schedules, questionnaire?
    How much originates – in the institution?
    – in the LEA?
    – from elsewhere?
    Are all staff involved? as individuals or groups?

APPENDICES 79

> Is there observation of lessons?
> Do pupils contribute? – parents? – employers?
> Are there external observers or consultants?
> To whom is the information available?

4. *How effective is the exercise?*

   What action has resulted?
   Has it led to improvements?
   Has the exercise been reviewed?
   Is fresh thinking apparent?
   What are the advantages, disadvantages and general effectiveness of the exercise in this school/college? (If possible, include reference to the cost (time/manpower etc) of the exercise.)

5. *Is there a written report? What form does it take?*

   What aspects of school life are reported on?
   What is the balance between description and evaluation?
   Is there reference to pupil outcomes?
   Is there reference to teacher performance?
   To whom does the report go?

6. *What is the time scale of the exercise?*

Aide-memoire used by HMI in relation to teacher appraisal

a. What appear to be the motives and purposes of these teacher assessment procedures?

   Primarily for HM'S use?
   Related to LEA requirements for accountability?
   Related to promotion possibilities?
   Related to school policies on – organisation?
                                      – curriculum?
                                      – staff development?

b. What is the scope of the assessment?

   What information is collected and recorded?
   What judgements are made?
   What are the criteria for the judgements?
   Who establishes the criteria?

c. What methods are used?

   Who is involved in making judgements?
   How was it presented to/perceived by teachers?
   Is there any input from others (ie not teachers)?
                    – inspectors?
                    – governors?
                    – pupils?
                    – parents?

d. What are the outcomes?

   Are there written records? (For whom?) (For how long are they kept?)
   What use is made of the assessment?
   Who is responsible for any consequent action?
   Is there any evidence to suggest that the process is improving, or is likely to improve, pupils' learning opportunities?

e. How effective is the operation?

   Have teachers been helped to assess their:

   classroom performance?
   relationships with pupils?
   lesson preparation?
   assessment techniques?

   Has the assessment of teachers' performance actually helped to improve it? (ie do the observations of teaching skills support any improvement which teachers/HM may claim to have occurred?)
   Are there other significant benefits?
   Are there particular problems?
   Is the exercise to continue?

APPENDIX B

CONFIDENTIAL

**University of Exeter
School of Education**

B.Ed. Teaching Practice Grade (School)

Student: .... Year: ....

School: ....

Will you please circle *one* letter to indicate the school's grade for the above student. Plus and minus signs or other qualifying remarks should *not* be added.

GRADES ...　　A　　B　　C　　D　　E

NOTES

1. The Final Teaching Practice Grade awarded is based on a five point scale (A–E), and E is a fail grade.

Grade A	The student performs excellently on most of the criteria and has weaknesses in few or none.
Grade B	The student performs excellently on some criteria and well on most of the others.
Grade C	The student performs very well on some criteria and satisfactorily on all or most of the others.
Grade D	The student performs satisfactory on some criteria and has weaknesses in several others.
Grade E	The student performs poorly on several criteria and is not yet competent to teach children.

2. The Final Teaching Practice Grade awarded by the University Examination Board will be arrived at by taking into account the written report and grade supplied by
   (i) the School,
   (ii) the University tutors, together with any observations by the external moderator.

University of Exeter
School of Education

B.Ed. Degree – Criteria for Teaching Practice

The criteria have been produced to provide guidance for teachers, tutors and students who are involved in teaching practice. It is recognised that the dimensions are by no means independent of each other but they nevertheless provide a checklist of the main skills involved in teaching. The levels described for each dimension represent stages in progression along that dimension; they require further interpretation in the light of the particular school circumstances.

MANAGEMENT AND TEACHING SKILLS

CATEGORIES	E ←——————— C ———————→ A		
1. RELATIONSHIPS WITH CHILDREN (including class control)	Poor. Lacks ability to secure attention from the class as a whole and withdraws from informal contact with children. Considerable difficulties with class control. Ignores children's responses.	Shows some ability to secure attention from the class as a whole and works satisfactorily with groups and individuals.	Is responsive to individuals as well as to the class as a whole. Obtains good control by encouragement and reception of ideas rather than by criticism and coercion, often successfully.
2. ORGANISATION	Lessons poorly organised with insufficient attention paid to beginnings and ends of lessons, organisation of groups, transitions from one activity to another and the availability and appropriateness of materials and equipment. Poor knowledge of school resources.	Lessons for the most part satisfactorily organised from beginning to end. Effective management of individuals, small groups, and class.	Changes class organisation smoothly to suit new activities. Employs varying teaching styles and strategies, and is willing to experiment.
3. SELECTION AND PRESENTATION OF MATERIAL	Material selected for presentation is usually unsuitable. Work set is usually too easy or too difficult or inappropriate. Few aids used.	Presentation of appropriately selected materials is clear, though characteristically safe rather than imaginative. Often fails to achieve fruitful exploitation of these materials through inability to foresee differing possibilities and set suitable tasks.	Shows initiative, inventiveness and skill in employing a variety of methods, including the use of teaching aids. Prescribes tasks which are closely adjusted to the age range and varying abilities of the children.
4. CHILDREN'S RESPONSE	Children inattentive and lacking in interest, generally apathetic and in some ways disruptive. Little or no improvement in children's responses during the practice.	Children's written and verbal responses and practical involvement variable but generally satisfactory. Improvement in level of children's response towards end of practice.	Children's response was spontaneous and their enjoyment obvious. Discussion of work often initiated by children's questions and children were disappointed when lesson ended.
5. CHILDREN'S PROGRESS	Children made no noticeable progress and in some cases the standard of their performance deteriorated. Student seemed unaware of children's lack of involvement or progress.	Progress satisfactory in the sense that the class teacher does not feel that the children have been held back. Student's assessment of children's progress is sporadic and short term rather than with an extended perception.	Children took a pride in their work realising much of their potential with a consistently high quality of performance. Clear evidence of perceptive monitoring of their progress by the student. School impressed by standard of work achieved.

PERSONAL AND PROFESSIONAL QUALITIES

CATEGORIES	E ←——————— C ——————→ A		
1. KNOWLEDGE	Inadequate knowledge of subject-matters for effective teaching.	Adequate knowledge of subject-matters for effective teaching.	Outstanding knowledge of subject-matters, contributing to highly effective teaching.
2. PLANNING AND PREPARATION	Inadequate. Plans set-piece schemes unrelated to the children's own experiences and capabilities.	Schemes and lessons generally well-planned with attention given to objectives, content, method and materials required. Has some difficulty in modifying preparation to meet changing circumstances.	Schemes and lessons carefully matched to children's abilities and interests. Flexible in approach and adapts plans to meet changing needs.
3. VERBAL AND NON-VERBAL SKILLS	Poor speech articulation, inappropriate vocabulary. Absence of modulation. Communication lacks expression.	Speech firm and clear. Vocabulary appropriate for children. Little variation in tone or voice or in use of gestures. Questioning technique clear but often unimaginative. Tends to give away information rather than leading children to it with appropriate questions and suggestions.	Employs a variety of verbal and non-verbal techniques which provoke enthusiastic and fruitful responses from the children.
4. EXTRA CURRICULAR ACTIVITIES	Minimal interest or involvement.	Becomes involved if asked but shows little initiative.	Very interested and keenly involved. Shows appropriate initiative.
5. INDIVIDUAL CHARACTERISTICS	This category covers all those personal characteristics which influence the quality of relationships in the classroom and staffroom, and include: Social rapport, Courtesy, Sensitivity, Reliability, Enthusiasm, Confidence, Open-mindedness, Responsiveness to Advice, Sense of humour, and Appearance.		

EVALUATION SKILLS

CATEGORIES	E ←——————— C ——————→ A		
1. EVALUATION AND RECORDING	Poor and irrelevant observations of children's behaviour. Work frequently carelessly marked or not marked. Little self-evaluation.	Interprets children's behaviour sensitively and sometimes accurately. Tries to keep abreast of marking and to keep appropriate records. Reflects on own teaching and makes adjustments.	Gives much thought to children's behaviour and responses and carefully monitors their progress. Conscientious over marking and record keeping. Very perceptive in evaluating own teaching.
2. TEACHING PRACTICE NOTEBOOK	Poorly presented with inadequate thought given to content, method or material. Few or superficial lesson appraisals. Evidence of failure to act on advice.	Acceptably presented notebook providing a documented record of work done. Some thought given to method as well as content and additional material added where appropriate. Lesson appraisals restricted in their perception but conscientious. Some evidence of response to advice.	Thorough preparation reflected in a well-presented and carefully arranged notebook. Schemes adapted to meet children's responses and needs. Lesson appraisals show considerable awareness and insight. Clear evidence of willingness and ability to respond to advice.

University of Exeter
School of Education

Final B.Ed. Teaching Practice Report

Student : .... Year : .... School : ....

Class/Age Range : .... Subjects : ....

Would you please report on the above student utilising the headings listed below.
The School Teaching Practice Grade should not be recorded on this report.

MANAGEMENT AND TEACHING SKILLS

1. RELATIONSHIPS WITH CHILDREN (including class control)
2. ORGANISATION
3. SELECTION AND PRESENTATION OF MATERIAL
4. CHILDREN'S RESPONSE
5. CHILDREN'S PROGRESS

PERSONAL AND PROFESSIONAL QUALITIES

1. KNOWLEDGE
2. PLANNING AND PREPARATION
3. VERBAL AND NON-VERBAL SKILLS
4. EXTRA-CURRICULAR ACTIVITIES
5. INDIVIDUAL CHARACTERISTICS

EVALUATION SKILLS

1. EVALUATION AND RECORDING
2. TEACHING PRACTICE NOTEBOOK

Signed .... Date ....

Bibliography

Barr, A.S., 1961, 'Wisconsin Studies of the Measurement and Prediction of Teacher Effectiveness', *Journal of Experimental Education*, 30, 5–156.

Bennett, N., Desforges, C., Cockburn, A. and Wilkinson, B., 1984, *The Quality of Pupil Learning Experiences*, Lawrence Erlbaum Associates, London.

Bridges, E.M., 1986, *The Incompetent Teacher*, Falmer Press, Lewes.

Delaney, P., 1986, *Teacher Appraisal in the Primary School*, Junior Education Special Report, Scholastic Press, Leamington Spa.

Department of Education and Science (DES), 1978, *Primary Education in England*, HMSO, London.

Department of Education and Science (DES), 1979, *Aspects of Secondary Education in England*, HMSO, London.

Department of Education and Science (DES), 1985, *Quality in schools: Evaluation and Appraisal*, HMSO, London.

Flanders, N.A., 1970, *Analysing Teaching Behaviour*, Addison-Wesley, New York.

Gage, N.L. 1978, *The Scientific Basis of the Art of Teaching*, Teacher College Press, New York.

Gray, J., Jesson, D. and Jones, B. 1986, *The Search for a Fairer Way of Comparing Schools' Examination Results*, Research Papers in Education, 1, 2, 91–122.

Guetzkow, H., Kelly, E.L. and McKeachie, W.J. 1954, 'An Experimental Comparison of Recitation, Discussion and Tutorial Methods in College Teaching', *Journal of Educational Psychology*, 45, 193–209.

Hamilton, D., 1975, *Handling Innovation in the Classroom: Two Case Studies in* W.A. Reid and D.F. Walker (eds) *Case Studies in Curriculum Change*, Routledge and Kegan Paul, London.

Hammersley, M. (ed), 1986 a, *Case Studies in Classroom Research*, Open University Press, Milton Keynes.

Hammersley, M. (ed), 1986 b, *Controversies in Classroom Research*, Open University Press, Milton Keynes.

Kounin, J.S., 1970, *Discipline and Group Management in Classrooms*, Holt, Rinehart and Winston, New York.

Macmillan Focus Series (see below)

Ryans, D.G., 1960, *Characteristics of Teachers*, American Council on Education, Washington D.C.

Samph, T., 1976, 'Observer Effects in Teacher Verbal Behaviour', *Journal of Educational Psychology*, 68, 6, 736–41

Suffolk Education Department, 1985, *Those Having Torches ... Teacher Appraisal: a Study*.

Suffolk Education Department, 1987, *In the Light of Torches ... Teacher Appraisal: a further Study*.

Whyte, J.B., 1986, *Teacher Assessment: a Review of the Performance Appraisal Literature,* Research Papers in Education, 1, 2, 137–163.
Wragg, E.C., 1981, *Class Management and Control,* Macmillan, Basingstoke.
Wragg, E.C., 1984, *Classroom Teaching Skills,* Croom Helm, London.
Youngman, M., 1984, *The Nature of the New Teacher's Job* in Wragg E.C. (1984) op.cit. pp 180–192.

FOCUS *workbooks* (Macmillan)

1981
E.C. Wragg *Class Management and Control*
T. Kerry *Teaching Bright Pupils in Mixed Ability Classes*

1982
P. Bell and T. Kerry *Teaching Slow Learners in Mixed Ability Classes*
T. Kerry and M.K. Sands *Mixed Ability Teaching in the Early Years of Secondary School*
T. Kerry *Effective Questioning*
G. Brown and N. Hatton *Explanations and Explaining*
T. Kerry and M.K. Sands *Handling Classroom Groups*
T. Kerry *The New Teacher*

Subject Specialist Series

1984
K.E. Selkirk *Teaching Mathematics*
J.D. Nichol *Teaching History*
T. Kerry *Teaching R.E.*
J.A. Partington and P. Luker *Teaching Modern Languages*

1985
M.K. Sands *Teaching Science*
C. Daniels and U. Hobson *Teaching Home Economics*
F.H. Molyneux and H. Tolley *Teaching Geography*
P. King *Teaching English*